Geoffrey Faulder

Spiffing Shrapnel

Memories of growing up in South London
during and after World War II

Mereo Books

2nd Floor, 6-8 Dyer Street, Cirencester, Gloucestershire, GL7 2PF
An imprint of Memoirs Books. www.mereobooks.com
and www.memoirsbooks.co.uk

SPIFFING SHRAPNEL

ISBN: 978-1-86151-912-2

First published in Great Britain in 2024
by Mereo Books, an imprint of Memoirs Books.

A CIP catalogue record for this book is available from the British Library.

The address for Memoirs Books can be
found at www.mereobooks.com

Mereo Books Ltd. Reg. No. 12157152

Typeset in 11/17pt Calisto
by Wiltshire Associates.
Printed and bound in Great Britain

SPIFFING SHRAPNEL

MEREO

CONTENTS

Introduction

Did you know that the difference between an ape and a monkey is that monkeys have tails, also that the Earth is roughly 4.6 billion years old and that human beings evolved in Africa between 6 and 2 million years ago and over time spread to cover the globe? That dinosaurs appeared 240 million years ago and became extinct 66 million years ago? Well now you do!

I am, by nature curious; I need to know how, when, where and why. They say curiosity killed the cat, but, so far as I am concerned, well done pussy, I'd rather die of curiosity than boredom or ignorance.

I am a 'Gemini'. Now, the rational part of me says this astrology business is far-fetched and superstitious 'hocus pocus', but when you consider the strong and vital effect the Moon's gravitational pull has on Earth, why not similarly the cosmos on us mere mortals? Anyway all I can say is that many years ago I had a professional astrologer give me a reading, then a little later a graphologist did the same on my handwriting. Weirdly the two readings, independently given by people who had minimal personal knowledge of my character, were very similar, so I don't know. I keep an open mind.

I love reading and literature, good literature (I'm a bit of a literary snob!) and am fascinated by words and their sounds. When asked who my favourite authors are, I am in a quandary as I enjoy so many but if pushed would say, inter alia, Dickens, Dostoyevsky, Donne, Hardy, Shakespeare, Steinbeck, Orwell. But there are many others. I suppose in short I like writers, not just spinners of a good yarn, although I love a good detective story and there are some great writers in this genre.

I also love steam locos and, tongue in cheek, tell people that the only lady I've been in love with all my life is a 'Duchess', which enthusiasts will know is a wonderful 4-6-2 Pacific loco designed in the late 30s by Sir William Stanier for the LMS. To me this loco is the epitome and the cherry on the cake of steam locos, although a 'Black Five' would run it close. Someone once described the allure of steam locos as being because they were the perfect example of kinetic sculpture having shape/form, movement, sound and smell. I'll go along with that.

Next in my list of passions is music, mainly jazz/swing and classical. So it ranges through Basie, Ellington, Armstrong, Goodman, Shaw, Bach, Mozart, Tchaikovsky and Verdi, just to name a few.

But it doesn't stop there folks, no. I am interested in just about everything from dinosaurs, the cosmos and all life forms, from insects to elephants and whales. Indeed natural history in general. Trees are a particular delight. So I hope you are getting an idea of what makes me me!

It's a funny thing about looking back and trying to remember things when you are my age, because events that occurred relatively recently are not as clear as things that happened way back in the early years of your life. Consequently my memories of things that happened during the war are as vivid in my mind as if they took place yesterday, whereas what happened last week is, to say the least, largely a blur!

Anyway I'm writing this account of my early life and times as a record of what I experienced and thought and liked which so influenced and shaped me. Also, it's a little self indulgent, as I love history.

A study of history, even a cursory one, will explain how we got to be where we are and who we are. and I don't just mean our own country's origins and past but the history of our world. I never cease to be surprised at the ignorance of the past displayed not only by the public at large, but perhaps more importantly politicians and world leaders. I am hoping therefore that my efforts here will inspire those who succeed me to continue the narrative of our family and lives, which will be of great interest I am sure to later generations.

It is a cause of some regret to me that my ancestors left no such accounts of their lives, loves and thoughts. How fascinating it would have been to have such a record. Instead, for the most part all we have is a collection of photographs, largely blank as to date, location and identification. In the family archive that I have built up I have therefore tried to annotate the photos accordingly. A significant part of my narrative concerning family and relatives is based on conversations I have had, or to which I was a party, with family and friends, and some is anecdotal. Although this makes it to a certain extent hearsay, I am confident it is pretty accurate. I am well aware that memory can and does play tricks and can easily embellish or diminish one's recollections and have taken care, so far as I can, to avoid such nuances.

In constructing this account of my life, I have tried to avoid a purely chronological 'cradle to dotage' narrative and used objects or events to try to bring events to life. Hopefully, this makes it more readable and interesting. I have also shared my thoughts on a variety of topics to give a flavour of who I really am.

So here we go!

CHAPTER 1

A wartime childhood

Once upon a time...

It's a cool, dark but starry night in autumn. A smartly dressed middle-aged woman walks quickly, purposefully, down Craignish Avenue, a pleasant tree-lined road in Norbury, one of South London's so called 'dreaming suburbs'. It's an avenue of smart semi-detached houses all with well tended front gardens, the epitome of 1930s middle England. Her shoes clip-clop on the pavement and she is clutching the hand of a little boy, almost dragging him along in her anxiety for some reason, to reach home a short distance away. It's quiet apart from the rumble of a distant electric train on the nearby main London to Brighton railway line. There are no street lights, so the only light is from the Moon.

Suddenly the stillness is shattered by the chilling wail of a warning siren, and its menacing, mournful sound prompts the woman to quicken her pace. Almost immediately searchlights pierce the dark skies and laser-like sweep the night sky, seeking to illuminate enemy bombers for the anti-aircraft or 'Ack-Ack' guns to shoot down. Straight away the guns open fire, hurling their high explosive shells up towards the approaching bombers, filling the air with loud cracks and rumbling bangs like a thunderstorm but deadlier, much deadlier. The drone of aircraft engines and the distant sounds of bombs exploding adds to the cacophony.

The woman and little boy are now running, desperate to get under cover. The aircraft are German bombers, the year is 1940, the woman is my mother, the little boy is me. My mother starts to run, pulling me along as fast as my little legs will let us, gripping my hand even tighter. I can sense, almost feel, her fear bordering on terror at being caught out in the open during an air raid. Yes, I had sort of known there was a war on and that people were frightened and apprehensive, but until now I had felt insulated from the reality of it and the very real threat of death or injury it posed.

Mother is now shouting for help as we dash down the road. Desperate to find shelter, we run into the front garden of one of the houses and Mother hammers frantically on the front door shouting for help, but there's no response. The house is blacked out and the occupants are either away or in their own air raid shelter, out of earshot.

We dash back into the road, Mother once more desperately shouting for help and knowing that just one piece of shrapnel from our own anti-aircraft gun shells could maim us both, or worse.

Then, suddenly out of the dark, a man appears running towards us, flashing a torch. 'Quick!' he says, 'this way, follow me'. We run behind him up a back alleyway and into his back garden, where he has a 'dug out' or Anderson shelter where his wife and daughter are sitting wrapped in blankets. Mother heaves a sigh of relief and visibly relaxes, glad that we are now under cover and relatively safe. She thanks the man profusely and starts to chat to his wife. I am tired and confused but happy now that I sense we are safe. Meanwhile, like a thunderstorm the sounds of the guns and aircraft gradually diminish as the raid passes over.

Some half an hour or so later the 'All clear' siren sounds to signal that the raid is over and Mother thanks everyone again and we make our way back to our home, a few hundred yards away in the next road.

Some good news at last

It's the morning of May 27th 1941, my third birthday. I'm sitting in an armchair in our back dining room by the fireplace watching Mother on her hands and knees blackleading the grate and its surround, then resetting the fire with newspaper and wood kindling. The wireless is on and it's a minute or so to nine o'clock. The 'pips' go to herald the nine o'clock news, which is read by Stuart Hibberd, at that time a famous BBC announcer.

Mother pauses in her work and listens attentively. The headline news is that Royal Navy battleships and Fleet Air Arm aircraft in the North Sea have located and sunk the biggest and perhaps most famous of German battleships, the *Bismarck*, pride of the German Navy, its most modern and heavily armed ship. Mother cheers and throws her arms in the air, looking flushed and excited. 'Come on!' she says and we go out into the front garden and join a throng of neighbours all chatting excitedly.

'Have you heard the news?' she says 'We've sunk the bloody *Bismarck!*'

Everyone nods approvingly and looks very happy. Earlier that month the *Bismarck* had sunk the famous British battleship HMS *Hood* with the loss of almost the entire crew of 1400 men. After months of gloom and bad news this is a rare moment to celebrate a signal victory.

The Allied air forces strike back

I am now four years old. It is late May 1942, about eight o'clock in the evening, and I'm in bed in the small front single bedroom of our house in Dunbar Avenue with the curtains drawn to keep out the fading light, in spite of which I am still lying awake. I struggle to fall asleep as I can hear the muffled sounds of people talking in the street below and the distant throbbing hum of a large number of aircraft rumbling across the twilight sky.

Gradually the sound of the aircraft gets louder, as do the voices of the people in the street, who seem animated and excited. Then I hear the sound of someone running up the stairs. My bedroom door opens and Mother comes in. 'Come on,' she says, 'you've got to see this'. I stand up on the bed and she wraps me in my father's dressing gown and carries me downstairs and out into the front garden. It seems like the whole road is out and gazing upward, scanning the darkening sky which is filled with swarms of aircraft of all types, mainly heavy and medium bombers plus some fighter escorts.

The hum of their engines has now become a roar. Some signal lights flash between the planes as they assume formations and turn south-east in great phalanxes towards Northern Europe.

I am witnessing the first 1000-bomber raid on Germany. After nearly three years of being bombed day and night by the Germans we are now dishing it out to them, giving them a taste of their own medicine. The German industrial towns and cities will be bombed and blasted as they have bombed and blasted ours.

The mood in the street among the people was quiet elation, but also a little sombre at the sight and sound of the awesome air armada that was overhead. Some people waved and clapped and shouted encouragement although of course none of the aircrew could see, let alone hear, what was happening in the streets below. It was a sobering thought that more than a few of the men above us would never return to their families and loved ones but instead become an inscription on a civic War Memorial somewhere.

Mother, still holding me, we craned our necks gazing up into the darkening sky for about twenty minutes as the bombers flew over on their deadly mission of death and destruction.

One of the women in the street, known as a bit of a busybody, said to Mother, 'Shouldn't he be in bed?' 'No' said Mother, 'I wanted him to see this, this is history.'

And so it was.

Flying bombs

Now it's high summer 1944. The large garden lawn in the back garden of our house at 15 Dunbar Avenue is parched brown in places and the ground is baked hard. Fruit is ripening on the apple and plum trees. It's after 10 in the morning, another bright, warm sunny day and all set for a hot one. I have constructed, or rather fashioned, a battle cruiser using a large wooden stepladder laid flat on the grass with a superstructure of various discarded household items retrieved from the outside toilet-cum-garden store, and a Union Flag flies from my broom handle flagstaff.

In spite of the weather, I'm wearing a navy blue child's overcoat with gold braid epaulettes and shiny brass anchor embossed buttons as befits my officer rank (no able seaman moi!) As captain, I am patrolling the Atlantic, hunting German U-boats which I destroy by hurling large clods of hard baked earth at the imagined targets, which on impact disintegrate, simulating an explosion in a most satisfying way.

Mother is standing at the kitchen sink looking through the window as she washes up the breakfast things, watching me and listening to the wireless. While I am so engaged in making the ocean safe for our ships, my attention is suddenly diverted to a strange sound rather like a motor cycle engine but coming from the sky – very odd. I look up and see what looks like a strange sort of aeroplane with smoke coming out the back of it with an occasional spurt of flame. It's flying quite low, only maybe a couple of thousand feet if that, and heading north towards London.

Excited, I shout and wave to Mother, 'Quick Mum, look, there's a plane on fire' She comes out of the kitchen door and stands on the back steps and looks up to where I am pointing. Almost immediately she shouts at me to come in quickly and runs towards me, grabs me and bundles me back into the house and into the back dining room, where we dive into the big solid steel Morrison shelter, close the mesh blast screen and lay down. Mother puts her arms around me and we wait anxiously. The 'plane' drones on into the distance, its engine getting fainter until we can hear it no more. After a while, we leave the shelter and continue where we left off.

It is August 1944, and the 'aeroplane' is a pilotless German V1 Flying Bomb, or 'Doodlebug' as they became to be known. When it runs out of fuel it will go into a dive, crash and its ton of explosive will detonate on impact, causing widespread death and destruction.

A note about the 'Doodlebug' and its successor. In all 6,725 V1 rockets were launched from sites in Holland against Britain, of which 2,340 hit London, causing 5,475 deaths and 16,000 injuries. Later, the more powerful, faster and longer range V2 rockets would be launched, carrying more explosive and travelling so fast they gave little or no warning until they struck. In effect they were the deadly fore-runner of the intercontinental ballistic missile.

My arrival

To go back to the beginning, I was born around 9 pm on 27th May 1938 in a private nursing home in Palace Road, Streatham, SW16. This of course was pre-NHS and my mother's confinement was overseen by our family doctor, Dr Ronald Anderson, a tall, rangy Scot with a wonderful personality and soft Scots accent. A few weeks later I was duly christened, as was the custom then, at a local church. My baptism certificate and photos of my christening party are in the archive

There are also some photos of me as a toddler in the back garden of our house, 15 Dunbar Avenue. Of course, I have no real memories until I was about three years old and these were of the war, which had broken out on 1st September 1939 when I was 16 months old. Because of the atmosphere and tension of those times, these memories have remained vivid to the present day, which I suppose is not surprising. I can still recall the chilling wail of the air raid warning siren, located on the roof of the local police station, signalling an impending German bomber raid.

These raids were usually at night and it was said that if you couldn't get to an air raid shelter, the safest place in a house was under the stairs. So in the early days before we were issued with a Morrison shelter, we would all squeeze together in the alcove under the stairs. There was Mother, me and Granny Stovold, Mum's mother, who was living with us, and Dad standing half in and half out. We would stay for maybe an hour or more until the raids were over when the siren sounded the 'All Clear', then we would all go upstairs to bed.

Later, I can't remember when, we were issued with a Morrison shelter, which was like a large steel table with a bed underneath and removable mesh blast screens which you put up once you were in.

The other type of shelter was the Anderson, which came as a kit which you erected away from the house in your back garden by digging a pit about the size of a double bed, lining it with corrugated sheeting so that half was below and half above ground and then piled the earth spoil from the pit over it. Of course neither type of shelter gave you complete protection, but they greatly improved your chances of survival, as was proved to be the case.

Without a doubt our Morrison shelter was the warmer and more comfortable of the two as the Anderson shelters, being outside, were colder and damper, although people did use paraffin heaters to warm them up.

All windows were 'blacked out' with blackout fabric or screens so that at night no light was visible to aid German bombers' navigation to their targets. The windows were also covered with criss-cross strips of tape to try and avoid too much flying glass in the event of a bomb blast. All vehicles also had to have hoods or shades over their headlights, which made night driving more dangerous. However there was of course far less traffic than in these days. Interestingly, a few vehicles were adapted to run on town gas, which meant they had a large fabric container of gas carried on the roof, but these were few and far between as the danger in an accident was obvious.

To enforce the blackout, wardens were appointed to patrol the streets, usually on a bike, and they wore tin helmets with the initials ARP painted on the front, standing for Air Raid Precautions, and you could be prosecuted for violating the regulations, although few were as people appreciated that the restrictions were for everybody's benefit. If they did see a light they would first shout 'Put that light out!' which became a bit of a catchphrase during the Blitz. If you didn't comply, they would knock on your door and make you cover any gaps in your blackout, with an implied threat of prosecution.

Another important article in every day life was the gas mask, one of which was issued to everyone, as in the early days of the war there was a real fear of Germans dropping poison gas devices as had been done in the First World War. You had to take them with you wherever you went outside and had to have them readily to hand indoors. They were like, in a way, diving masks made of rubber with a circular filter attached to the end to neutralise the gas. You put them on over your head and adjusted the rubber casing straps to make them air tight and off you went. There were special 'Micky Mouse' ones for children (which I had) which were red and had a sort of nose on them, and there was even a cot-shaped one for babies. I found them a little claustrophobic and they tended to 'steam up'. Fortunately, they were never used, as no such raids occurred, but we would have been ready if one did!

One of the important things that people who weren't there don't know was that one of the major hazards during an air raid was falling shrapnel, fragments of steel from exploding shells from our own ant-aircraft guns. These were usually about four or five inches long and about an inch or so wide and half an inch thick with jagged edges made of solid steel, so quite chunky. When anti-aircraft gunners fire their shells they hope that even if they don't get a direct hit, which was seldom, then the blast of fragments from the exploding shell would seriously damage the aircraft. So if you were out in the open in the wrong place it could rain metal chunks on you, which could kill or maim you.

After raids it was common to see youngsters scouring the streets for shrapnel specimens, which were collected as a wartime hobby. I had a small collection myself and you could do swops of bits with friends to enhance your collection. I remember one of my school friends saying what a 'spiffing collection of shrapnel' he had, 'spiffing' being a slang word of the time, I suppose equivalent nowadays to 'brilliant'.

Cigarette cards were another favourite thing to collect. Most packets of cigarettes sold then contained a colourful card with information on the back covering a whole range of subjects depending on the manufacturer, including famous sportsmen, animals, steam locos, in fact any subject you can think of. They were a sales inducement, as each issue had up to 50 or so separate cards and each pack of cigarettes sold contained one or two cards.

As mentioned, my mother's widowed mother was living with us, her husband, Ernest Stovold, having died of diabetes in the1930s. Although in her 60s, she was still working as a sales assistant at a drapers, Rogers in Streatham High Street and each weekday morning she would set off at a brisk pace down the road to catch the 133 bus into work, sometimes puffing on a cigarette. Neighbours often remarked how full of energy she was for her age.

My father was a senior bank clerk at the Westminster Bank's Newington Butts branch, or Elephant & Castle as it was better known. He had joined the bank from school and worked there all his life. He didn't progress beyond the rank of 'clerk in charge,' a sort of relief manager, almost entirely due, I later learned, to my mother not wishing to move home, which meant when an opportunity for promotion arose elsewhere in the country he invariably had to decline it if offered and was thus passed over and eventually not considered for such opportunities.

At the outbreak of war he joined the LDV, or Local Defence Volunteers – the 'Home Guard' as it eventually came to be known – and he would report for duty each evening after work. One of his duties was to guard the local telephone exchange building, but later, around 1943 I think, he volunteered for the Regular Army, even though being over 40 he was otherwise exempt from conscription. He joined the Royal Artillery and was trained as a gun plotter responsible for issuing target orders to the field guns, which were 25-pounders. He was thus away most of the time training and then joined the D-Day invasion of Europe, going across, I believe, on D-Day plus six or thereabouts, and was almost immediately involved in the important strategic battle for Caen. Thus I saw very little of him until the war was over and he was demobbed in 1945.

We had very good neighbours in our road, and just to mention the ones we had most contact with, next door at 17 were Reg and Bess Larbey. Reg was a signalling instructor for the Southern Railway at Clapham Junction station, and Bess's mother 'Creff' lived with them, a sweet old lady but rather frail. On the other side at no 13 were Mr and Mrs Cross and their two sons, one of whom was in the Royal Navy, one in the RAF. They were a very cheery down to earth family, but I cant remember what Mr Cross did.

At no 21 lived Miss Frampton or 'Fram' as she was known, a spinster, who before retirement had been Head Milliner at Swan and Edgar, one of the premier stores in London's West End, now long gone and forgotten. She and Mother got on well, and as she was on her own with no relatives in the area, Mum suggested she pool some of her ration coupons with us, which would enable Mum to buy larger amounts of food, in exchange for which Fram would come round regularly for lunch with us. This worked very well. Fram had a quite cultured but loud and penetrating voice which became a bit wearing at times, particularly when she and I would have an argument over something, not serious, more a disagreement, but it could be quite noisy, which would provoke Mum to say 'for Christ's sake you two be quiet, I can't hear myself think!'

Some time after the war in 1946 when things were starting to get back to normal, Swan & Edgar asked Fram if she would help in making the hats for the Royal Ascot season as they were short of skilled staff for this important event in the fashion calendar. They sent the modelling blocks and material down to Fram by taxi and she set to work. But, she needed a model to help her get the designs right, so she asked Mum to act as a model for her. Mother was thrilled to do this and effectively previewed a lot of the fashionable hats to be worn by society ladies at Ascot that year.

Across the road were Mr and Mrs Wadey and their two children Joyce and Peter. Joyce was my age, but Peter was a year or so older. From time to time, particularly in the summer, they would come over and play with me in our garden or I would play in theirs. The Wadeys were staunch Methodists and regular churchgoers at the local Methodist church at Pollards Hill. However, as mum used to say, they aren't 'bible punchers' and don't mention their religion unless asked. After the war I did go at their behest to Sunday

School, but I soon got fed up with it and pleaded with my parents not to make me go, and they eventually agreed.

However, back to wartime. Now my mother was a very feisty lady and although quick tempered she was equally quick to cool down and never sulked, as she hated sulking. She was respected by the local tradesmen and woe betide the shopkeeper who tried to pass off inferior goods to her. Having said that, she could be a very staunch and loyal friend, generally much liked by everybody, and was always ready to help those in genuine need. She was, and remained all her life, a 'true blue' Conservative. She never referred to the Labour Party without the prefix 'bloody'!

An example of this feistiness which I well remember occurred around 1942/3. It was a warm summer's day and all the doors and windows were open when suddenly we heard the sound of someone singing a hymn, shortly followed by a knock at the front door. 'Who the hell is that?' said Mother under her breath, looking at me. I followed her to the front door, where standing on the doorstep with a portable wind-up record player were two young men, as it turned out Americans. One of them said 'Good morning Ma'am, we have come to bring you the Lord's message'. They announced themselves as from the Mormon Church or maybe Jehovah's Witnesses or some such.

Mother glared at them and said 'Oh really, and how old are you?' 'Twenty [something]' they replied.

'Well why aren't you in the bloody army fighting bloody Hitler like my husband who's over 40?' she said. 'Now bugger off or I'll throw your bloody record player over the fence.' She advanced menacingly towards them. Needless to say they beat a hasty retreat, much to the amusement of our neighbour, Bess Larbey, who had been watching the episode. She said, 'That's right Madge, you tell 'em!'

'Don't worry, I bloody well will,' said Mother.

CHAPTER 2

Oxford days

For a brief period, some time around 1944 I think, Mother took me to stay with my Aunt Phil and her daughter Jean, my cousin, in Oxford to get away from the bombing.

At the outbreak of war, in order to keep children safe, the Government had arranged an evacuation scheme whereby all children of school age were evacuated to various parts of the country deemed to be less prone to bombing. Children were labelled, and with just a small case with their clothes and personal effects despatched by train to various parts of the country, where they were billeted on volunteer families. They stayed there until the end of the war.

As I was too young I wasn't involved in this scheme and stayed at home, but because of the bombing and increasing V1 attacks it was felt I should be moved to the country anyway, and Uncle Ken and Aunt Phyllis' place was the obvious choice. Phyllis was my dad's brother's wife and they lived in Alexandra Road, off Botley Road in Oxford. Dad's brother, Uncle Ken, was in the RAF transport section. He was a superb motor engineer and had worked at the Morris Motors factory in Cowley. Cousin Jean was two or three years older than me, but we got on all right, although I think she tolerated me then rather than liked me. Years later we engaged in regular correspondence, as she liked to receive my letters, particularly after her husband Mick died. We shared a love of books, and when she left school she got a job at the world famous Bodleian Library in Oxford.

Aunt Phil was a lovely lady and quite religious, treating me like her own, and in the circumstances I was quite happy there in spite of missing my mother, who would come up to see me when she was able to. We were no more than a couple of hundred yards from the countryside and the rivers where we would go walking, on many occasions sometimes on my own. You wouldn't dream of allowing that these days but then no one thought it dangerous in spite of the proximity of some large rivers.

My overall memories of my time in Oxford (2 Alexandra Road, Botley Road) are happy ones. I particularly liked wandering along the river banks and looking for fish and birds. There are two main rivers in Oxford, the Thames of course being the major one, and the Cherwell. Both had a number of smaller tributaries, some of which were within easy walking distance of the house.

I remember there was a large pool on one of the small rivers that was big enough to swim and dive into and it had a small diving board. At that time however I was a non-swimmer, so I just paddled in the shallows. I did however love to 'fish' for sticklebacks and other small fish using a jam jar with a long piece of string tied around the neck which I filled with bait, usually small bits of bread. I would drop it into the river and wait for the fish to swim in, then quickly yank it out. After watching the fish for a while I would return them to the river.

However, familiarity breeds contempt. On one occasion I was fishing off a very grassy bank which was a bit damp and slippery. While attempting to cast my jam jar into the river, I slipped and plunged straight into the water over my head. Fortunately I was able to surface quickly and heave myself out up the bank, albeit shivering, partly with shock, partly with cold, as it was a cool autumn day.

Cold, soaked to the skin and crying, I ran home. At the end of the road where we lived there was a recreation ground with football pitches and in spite of a match being in progress I ran straight across one of them, much to the amusement of the lads playing, who laughed at me and made fun of my predicament, much to my annoyance.

I finally reached home and in floods of tears hammered on the front door, which was opened by a startled Aunt Phil, who read my situation at a glance and ushered me into the parlour, where a coal fire was burning in the grate. She undressed me and towelled me dry in front of the fire, then gave me a glass of water and an Aspirin, which I immediately spat out. Through my tears and sobs I declared, 'I'm never going near that bloody river again!' Poor Aunt Phil a very proper Christian lady was completely taken aback by my language and remonstrated with me to this effect. However, in the warm parlour I soon regained my composure and said sorry and was forgiven.

On reflection, who these days would allow a five- or six-year-old out alone in the country, let alone one with so many rivers? But these are very different times. Then it was quite common to let children loose for a few hours and while tragedies did occur they were few and far between. We enjoyed a wonderful freedom, something of which today's cosseted youngsters have little or no experience. To be fair, there were then far fewer predatory males or weirdos than seems to be the case these days.

For as long as I can remember I've been fascinated by rivers and lakes and ponds, I can't really explain why, anymore than I can explain my love of the countryside, particularly trees and woods, which I think most of us have. Indeed, I've been a member of the Woodland Trust for about forty years and find great peace and tranquillity in woods, rather like being in a church, or better still a cathedral. Trees seem to have this rather regal, majestic quality and of course, as we now appreciate, they are vital to the environment as 'fixers' of CO2.

So it wasn't long before the memory of my 'ducking' faded and I was back with my jam jar fishing for sticklebacks, although being a little more cautious about slippery banks!

While in Oxford I started at an infants' school, which was nearby in Botley Road or thereabouts, I can only vaguely remember this and wasn't there long before I went home. But I do remind people, tongue in cheek, that I was part educated at Oxford!

On the whole Jean and I got along quite well. She could be a bit bossy and made fun of me from time to time, but nothing upset me particularly. However, I do remember on one occasion when my dear sweet cousin with whom I shared the front double bedroom really embarrassed me. We had separate beds of course, but we would discreetly undress in the bedroom. One particular night I was trying to get out of my underpants and into my pyjamas without the slightest chance of my private parts coming into my cousin's prying eyes when suddenly she shouted with great glee, 'I saw it, I saw it!'

'No you didn't, no you didn't!' I said, blushing like a beetroot and diving into bed as Aunt Phil came up to quieten things down, put the light out and shut the door.

'I saw it,' whispered Jean from under the bedclothes. 'Didn't!' I spat back. 'Did, did, did!' she said. 'Didn't, didn't, didn't!' I said and stuck my head under my pillow.

I finally got my own back when eventually I left to go back home with mother, as I had become quite homesick and after due consideration it was decided on balance that it would be better for me to return home.

In the bedroom we both shared there was a very large heavy

Victorian double wardrobe with ornate carvings and inset with mirrors and decorative glass. I knew Jean thought it a bit spooky, and her bed was closest to it.

When the time came for me to leave, Mother told me to go upstairs to say goodbye to Jean, who was in the bedroom. I went upstairs and quietly opened the door, which made Jean jump as she had been immersed in a book. 'Bye' I said somewhat awkwardly. 'Bye' she replied.

Then I had a thought. 'You see that wardrobe,' I said' Yeees,' she drawled.

'Well there's an eye in there and it looks at you when you're asleep,' I said.

Cousin Jean freaked out. 'Mum!' she yelled. 'MUUUUM!'

I left with a satisfied smirk on my face. We often laughed about it in later years.

Jean eventually left school and got a job as a trainee librarian at the world famous Bodleian Library in Oxford, where she met her husband to be, Mick Dudley, who worked in the University photographic department. They moved to Great Milton just outside Oxford and bought a ramshackle old cottage which had the village church on one side and a large country house on the other. Some years later the country house became Le Manoir des Quatre Saisons, Raymond Blanc's famous restaurant. They had two children. Serena, who trained as a children's nanny, married an American Air force policeman and moved to the USA. The other, Jonathan, was a quiet reserved boy who never left home and was a nice lad but a bit a trifle eccentric and a confirmed bachelor.

In later years Jean and I regularly corresponded, as she loved to receive and send letters and I have kept some of hers in the archive.

Although I was reasonably happy with Auntie Phil and Jean in Oxford, I was quite homesick and on one occasion became quite upset when Mum left to return home.

Now where we lived in Norbury, South London was slap bang in the middle of what was known as 'Doodlebug Alley', lying along the regular route of V1 German pilotless bombers en route to London. A number of them fell short, demolishing houses and killing and maiming, so it didn't seem sensible to take me back until the bombing had ended. However, although it was questioned as to whether it was wise to take me back there, Mother decided almost on the spur of the moment, I think, that I would be happier with her, so she took me back home.

We arrived home about lunchtime and Mum's brother, Uncle Les, on leave from the Merchant Navy, was at the front garden gate looking out for us as we walked up the road.

'You bloody fool,' he said to Mother, 'Why have you brought him back here?'

'Ah well' she said, 'If we go, we'll go together.'

He sighed, shook his head and we all went indoors, where he was preparing lunch.

I often wonder how people today would have coped in those dangerous, very stressful times. On the basis of the prevalence of stress and mental illness these days when there is no immediate risk to life and limb, the answer would surely be not very well. However it is never sensible to underestimate the hidden reserves of courage and tenacity which lurk in the human breast, so maybe they would find the inner strength to confront their adversity and, as people did then, "press on regardless".

There are many anecdotes illustrating the indomitable spirit of ordinary people during the Blitz, but my favourite is about the 70-year-old lady in the East End of London. After a heavy air raid she was eventually dug out from under the debris of her home by the rescue squad and emerged covered in dust, her clothing torn and although much shaken and having sustained cuts and bruises, by some miracle, not seriously injured. Thanking her rescuers, she then became very agitated about having lost her handbag and insisted that it should be searched for. To placate her, a search among the wreckage was made and her rather bulky handbag found which she seized and opened. With a cry of 'Thank Gawd!' she produced an intact half bottle of Scotch whisky, much to her obvious relief. Whereupon one of her rescuers said, 'Go on ma, have a swig'. 'Not bleedin' likely' said the old lady, 'I'm saving this for an emergency'!

A V1 'Doodlebug' German flying bomb

Barrage balloons - very large hydrogen filled balloons tethered by steel wires and lown high enough to protect potential ground targets from enemy aircraft. A common sight during the war.

Child's gas mask

Morrison shelter, for use inside the house

Anderson shelter, for the garden

Cars adapted to run on town gas

CHAPTER 3

The tide turns

Victory in Europe

As the Allied Armies advanced further across Europe and into Germany, they overran and destroyed the V1 'Doodlebug' launch sites and their reign of terror was ended. However, as mentioned earlier, the Germans had perfected what turned out to be the first inter-continental ballistic missile. This was the more deadly V2 rocket which flew at three times the speed of sound or more than 2,000 miles per hour. It therefore gave no warning, or very little, of its approach. The first one was first launched on 8th September 1944, falling on a house in Chiswick and killing the occupants. The last fell on 27th March 1945, killing the occupants of a house in Orpington, Kent. In all V2s killed an estimated 2,750 civilians and injured another 6,523.

This rocket, developed by a team of top German scientists, headed by Werner von Braun, was later to become the basis on which the American space programme was built, the Americans having captured von Braun and persuaded him to continue his work in the USA.

By now the Nazi Third Reich was on its knees, with Allied armies advancing from the west and our Russian allies advancing from the east. Hitler committed suicide in his bunker in Berlin and

Germany surrendered unconditionally on 8th of May 1945. The nightmare was finally over.

There was a tremendous outpouring of joy and relief in the whole country and there were street parties and dancing in the streets. Flags and bunting were put up everywhere, it seemed, and there was a sort of carnival atmosphere. Our house was no exception and Mum got Uncle Les, who was home at the time, to decorate ours. But when she came out to inspect the decorations, she demanded Les remove the red Russian flag. 'But they are our allies,' said Les. Mother was adamant. 'Get that bloody red rag down!' she said, so down it came.

There's a photo of Mum, Nan Stovold, Miss Frampton and me at the front garden gate in the archive. May 8th 1945 was declared 'VE Day' (Victory in Europe). However the War in the Far East against Japan continued against stubborn and fanatical Japanese resistance. It was finally ended by the Americans dropping the first two atomic bombs on Hiroshima and Nagasaki with enormous loss of life and injury, killing 120,000 civilians. The war officially ended on the 2nd September 1945 with the unconditional Japanese surrender.

Looking back, what did this war achieve? The answer of course is that it destroyed a brutal, sadistic German dictatorship and thwarted the territorial ambitions of an equally ruthless Japanese military regime. But victory came at a huge cost in lives and property and produced a deep feeling of bitterness and suspicion of Germany and Japan in particular.

However time, the great healer, has run its course and we are now happily on excellent terms with both countries, and have a thriving trade with them. Indeed UK roads are full of German and Japanese cars and lorries, some of which are even manufactured in the UK.

The post World War 2 conflicts in Korea and Vietnam have

likewise achieved nothing. Indeed history, especially in more modern times, shows how futile war has become and how it is best avoided as far as possible. However with people like Putin, power crazy political leaders and religious fanatics seeming to thrive on hatred and lying propaganda, suppressing freedom of speech, the world is presently as dangerous a place as ever.

Just imagine for a moment what our world would be like if all people and nations helped each other and looked to find common ground on which to cooperate instead of looking to exploit their differences. Dream on, Geoffrey!

Dad's war

From about 1943 my father was away serving in the army, having volunteered in spite of being over 40, which would otherwise have made him ineligible for service. He was drafted into the Royal Artillery and was trained as a gun plotter. This entailed him working in the Command Post, usually a tent or a commandeered property, where he would receive information from forward observation posts on enemy positions. For these he plotted the range and charge load of the shells, which he communicated to the batteries of 25-pounder field guns, then the principal artillery weapon of the British Army.

Dad didn't speak much about his wartime escapades until many years later, like most veterans of conflict. He landed on 'Gold' beach in Normandy on 23rd June 1944, a fortnight after D Day on June 6. June 1944, and almost immediately went into action in the bloody and protracted battle for Caen. His battery of 25-pounder field guns was assigned the role of a 'Flying Column' whose job it was to move quickly to support and reinforce Allied troops who were coming under heavy German fire.

He told me that on a number of occasions the guns were firing

24 hours non-stop until the gun barrels became white hot, when they had to be stood down for obvious safety reasons.

Very often, he told me, they had to go and dig American units out of trouble. On one such occasion he was with a small group of men going in to set up a command post in a small town when the came across an American General sitting on some steps, head in hands. He looked up at Dad and said 'Who the hell are you?' Dad saluted and said 'British field artillery sir'. 'Thank Christ for that,' said the General. 'Welcome to the party!'

Another incident that he told me about happened towards the end of the war. Dad was in a Jeep with an officer and two others driving into a small German town to 'recce' and set up a command post. As they approached the town they met a group of American soldiers who assured them the town had been evacuated by German troops. So imagine their surprise when on driving down a narrow street they came into the town square, where about a hundred German soldiers were lined up on parade!

The officer in Dad's Jeep ordered the driver to stop beside the German officer in charge. He then got out with his pistol at the ready and told the German to surrender immediately, a heart-stopping moment. Much to their surprise and relief the German officer complied without any protest or reaction and the troops laid down their weapons and apparently happily surrendered. Dad found out later this was because most German soldiers knew the end was nigh and further fighting was pointless. They wanted to surrender to the Allied American and British armies, who they knew would honour the Geneva Convention and treat them humanely. They knew the Russians, on the other hand, hated them with a vengeance, due to the atrocities and slaughter of Russians in the German invasion of Russia. It was known that the Russians would happily shoot prisoners in reprisal for this or they would be imprisoned in Siberia and probably be left to die of starvation and the cold. So when the opportunity arose they almost thankfully gave themselves up to the British or American Forces.

While they were collecting the weapons from the German troops, Dad noticed one of his comrades walking through the German ranks holding his beret, which contained the watches of some of the prisoners. Dad asked him what he was doing and he said 'Just liberating some gold timepieces, Don!' He gave Dad a couple. Later when I was older Dad gave me one to wear on special occasions.

Dad finally finished up in the town of Wismar on the Baltic, where the British and Americans finally met up with the advancing Russian or 'Red' Army. Prior to this they had been camped at Celle, a few miles from the notorious Bergen Belsen concentration camp where many Jews were imprisoned and executed. Only a few specialist troops were allowed in to deal with the dreadful situation that existed there with corpses piled high and emaciated, starving people barely alive. Dad said you could smell it even though it was a few miles from them.

One day while they were camped at Wismar, near the Russians, Dad met one of his unit walking over to the Russian lines with a jerry can of petrol. Dad asked where he was going and he said 'To trade with the Russkies'. Dad pointed out that petrol was no good to them as their tanks and vehicles were all diesel. 'No it's not for that,' he said,'they drink it mixed with fruit juice!' Now this seemed a bit unlikely, but from what we now know it is quite possible in the circumstances.

While he was in the army abroad advancing across Europe, Dad would send home presents and souvenirs. I remember he sent Mum a silks and cottons cum sewing box from, I think, Holland and I received a wonderful model Dutch two-masted sailing boat, more of which later. He also sent me a fantastic metal model of a German JU 87 dive bomber and a German pilot's fleece-lined flying helmet which had laryngaphones attached. These consisted of two pads attached to the sides of the helmet which were fastened across the throat to pick up vibrations from the larynx and convert them into speech. This was my pride and joy, but after a few months the helmet disappeared and I only discovered later that Mum had disposed of it on the pretext that 'those bloody Germans are flea ridden!'

Another item that Dad brought back was a copy of the Rubaiyat of Omar Khayyam. He got this in bizarre circumstances when he and another comrade stumbled onto a German dugout with two dead Germans in it, killed by shell blast, and this book, which I still have, lying nearby.

One other thing I remember in this vein was receiving two beautifully made balsa wood models of a Lancaster bomber and an American Kittyhawk fighter. These were given to my by Wilf, who stayed with us a couple of times. He came from Biggleswade in Bedfordshire, but I never did quite understand how we came to know him; I think he was in farming or agriculture, but they were terrific models which I prized.

Dad was eventually demobbed and returned home in 1945, although I can't quite remember which month. I remember him coming home and me being slightly in awe of him as effectively I had not had a father around for more than two years at a very formative time of my life. However, Dad was a very kind and gentle man and life fairly soon got back to normal. In my archive there is a small bound book, a diary of his unit's progress during their time in Europe throughout the war.

My father somewhere in Germany, 1944-5

The author, somewhere in Oxford

With cousin Jean, somewhere In Oxford

Mother, c1930

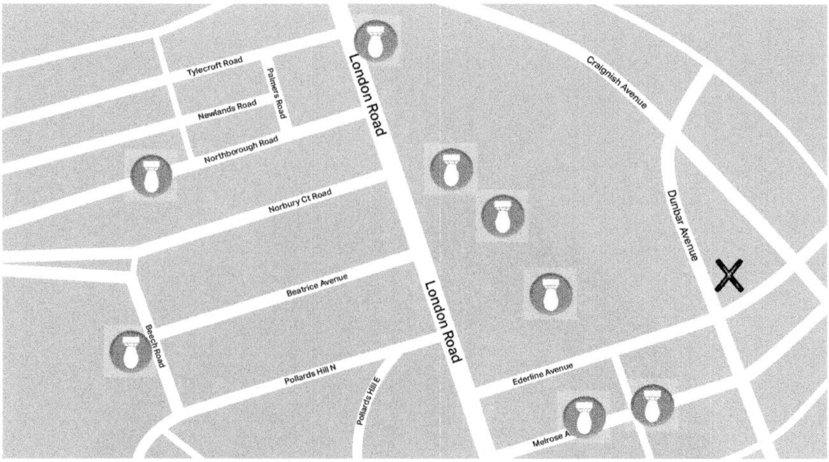

'Bombsight' map of bombs that fell near us (no 15 marked with a +)

Outside no 15 on VE Day, 8th May 1945 - Gran Stovold, me, Mother, Miss Frampton

25-pounder field guns

CHAPTER 4

The post-war years

The house we lived in at 15 Dunbar Avenue Norbury SW16 was a 1920s suburban semi-detached end of terrace house with a good size front garden and large back garden comprising a rectangular lawn, flower beds and about seven or eight mature fruit trees, apple, plum and greengage. There was an area of concrete outside the back door about 15' by 8' and a ramshackle brick coal shed. There were two double bedrooms, a single, a bathroom and downstairs a reception room or lounge, a dining room and a large kitchen with a coke boiler. The large downstairs rooms each had a grate for a coal fire. It was rented by my parents, the landlord being a Mr Hayden, a man in his 50s I think, shortish and slim with a moustache. Mother thought he looked like Dr Crippen, the notorious murderer, and didn't like him at all. She especially disliked his habit of coming into the house and not taking his hat off, which then was the polite thing to do, and I feel uncomfortable when I see men wearing hats indoors to this day.

Anyway on one memorable occasion he came round to collect the monthly rent and as usual came in with his trilby on. Shortly after, my Uncle Les, on leave from the Merchant Navy, came to the front door. Mum let him in but said 'Les, keep your hat on and go and say hallo to Hayden in the front room'. Slightly puzzled, Uncle Les did as he was asked and went in and exchanged pleasantries with our landlord. A few minutes later Mother stormed in, looked at Les and with one swift swipe of her hand knocked his hat off, at the same time saying 'Don't you know a gentleman takes his hat off when he enters a house?' Les apologised and Mr Hayden quickly snatched his trilby off, looking somewhat embarrassed. Mother and Les had a good laugh about it afterwards, but that was Mother!

In the late forties or early fifties my father brought the house as a sitting tenant for £400, which was a fairly large sum in those days. When they were first married they had rented a house in nearby Ederline Avenue, and moved to Dunbar Avenue around the time I was born.

The land the houses in the area were built on had been orchards, hence the large number of trees in our garden and those of our neighbours. When I was about eight I moved into the larger back bedroom and in the summer when you looked out of the window, you looked out on a sea of foliage, trees and shrubs and flower beds, almost rural if you ignored the serried rows of terraced houses that bordered the outer edges of the green oblong that constituted the back garden area of all the houses. About a quarter of a mile away as the crow flies was the main London to Brighton railway line of the Southern Railway. The passenger trains were mainly electric of course, running on the three-rail electrification system unique to the SR, as it was known. But, of course these were still the days of steam engines, so there were the regular steam-hauled express passenger trains to Newhaven and many freight or 'goods' trains.

One of my fond memories is of lying in bed on a winter's night with the rain beating on the windows and listening to the clank-clank of the goods trains as they laboured along the track, accompanied by the chugging of the locos hauling them. As I snuggled under my blankets it was somehow a comforting and reassuring sound. I used to imagine how wonderful it must be to be on the footplate steaming through the night and shovelling the coal in. Little did I know then what hard physical work it is, until I did one of my steam loco driving courses in later years.

My fascination and love of steam locomotives first manifested itself when I was in a pram. Whenever we got anywhere near the London-Brighton railway line bridge over the road at Manor Farm Road I would insist on stopping until at least one steam train went by. I would create if I was wheeled away!

During the war, to ensure we had a plentiful supply of eggs, we got some chickens. Some we bought, others we hatched from a clutch of fertile eggs and a broody hen, or in an incubator, until the chicks emerged, which was amazing and instructive. A suitable chicken house and run was acquired and installed at the bottom of the garden and after having their wings clipped, the chickens were let out to wander around the garden foraging for food as they would in their natural state. We had a variety of hens, seven or eight at any one time, either Light Sussex, Buff Orpington or Rhode Island Red.

On one occasion, we got a broody Buff Orpington hen to sit on a clutch of eggs and hatch some chicks, about ten or so I think. However, somehow or other one of the Light Sussex chicks turned out to be a bantam cock. He matured into a magnificent specimen with predominantly black plumage and very feisty – a true cock of the walk – and could be quite vicious with his beak and claws. We named him 'Blackie' and Mother managed to tame him. In the end she was the only one he would allow in his 'run' without attacking them.

So we had a plentiful supply of eggs during the war and into peacetime. Each day the surplus eggs were dated with a pencil and immersed in an isinglass preservative mixture in a bucket in the larder.

We finally gave up the chickens in the late forties, when eggs became easily obtainable in the shops, and Mother was relieved of the chore of preparing their one meal a day of boiled potato peelings mashed up with bran.

I think it was sometime during the late forties or early fifties when it was decided to dig a pond in the garden, which was done by Uncle Les on one of his leaves. It was an irregular sort of oval shape, one side being against a fence, the other on the lawn side with a small concrete path along its edge. Les dug a hole about two feet deep in the middle and lined it with concrete reinforced with mesh from the old Morrison shelter blast screens, the shelter having been taken back by the authorities for scrap.

When it was filled with part tap water, part rainwater, a water lily and weed were planted, and after a few weeks wildlife appeared, such as dragonflies, water beetles and to our great delight, newts. Before the lily and the weed spread I sailed some small model boats on it, but later I took great pleasure in sitting quietly beside it watching the wildlife, particularly the newts. We had Palmate newts and Great Crested, which were like miniature dragons or crocodiles.

The garden was a wonderful safe play area for me and my friends up to the age of 12 or 13. There were, as I have mentioned before, a large number of apple and plum trees, which were quite large and fun to climb. The lawn was just about big enough to play cricket or football if you were careful not to hit or kick the ball over the fence onto a neighbour's garden. Although on the odd times this happened they were generally quite forgiving, provided you apologised and grovelled a bit!

Among our neighbour were Mr and Mrs Roberts and their son Howard, who lived next door but one. Howard was a bit delicate and something of a 'mummy's boy', but we got on all right. His father worked for an oil company, and I remember being very envious of Howard when his parents bought him a large Hornby

Dublo train set which was set up on a permanent baseboard in their conservatory.

Later, as a present for passing the Eleven Plus, my parents bought me the Hornby Dublo Duchess of Atholl LMS express passenger train set with an oval of track. This to me was the best present ever and it was soon added to with points and sidings, and all the paraphernalia of railway furniture. As steel was in short supply after the war, track, points and wagons were in short supply and thus in high demand. When news got out that Hammonds, the local toy shop, had received a stock of these highly desirable items, there was a rush to buy them before they sold out. My pocket money then was half a crown a week, twelve and a half pence in today's money, but of course worth a heck of a lot more then. A set of points, for example, was seven and sixpence, or about thirty-five pence today. So there was much begging and pleading for parents to make up the shortfall on an earnest promise to repay them. I well remember my mother searching her purse for any extra money she could spare me.

All in all, in spite of Adolf Hitler, I had a very happy childhood in, as they later came to be known, 'the dreaming suburbs'.

One incident occurred which I have never forgotten. It was decided that we would have a dog, much to my excitement and delight, and we duly acquired a chocolate Labrador-type puppy, Bruce, whom I loved. Unfortunately he had not been neutered and one day he ran across the road and started to try and 'hump' a little girl out walking with her father. Although Mother managed to get hold of him, the girl's father was furious and made all sorts of threats. When my father came home and heard about it, it was decided he would have to go and he was duly taken to the local vet to be 'put to sleep'. This would almost certainly not happen nowadays, but it was different then. Needless to say I could not understand why this had to be and was very upset and very unhappy for some time. I never forgot him.

Animals have interested me ever since I can remember. One incident which I remember very well was my first visit to London Zoo when I was about eight and the Zoo had reopened after the war, during which most of the animals had been evacuated to Whipsnade and other zoos outside London. While we were walking around I was enthralled to see all the animals, such as camels, elephants, lions, giraffes etc. Then Dad and Uncle Les, who had taken me, pointed to a zebra and said "what's that, Geoff?"

I thought for a moment then said "It's a donkey in a football shirt". This made Dad and Les convulse with laughter, much to my annoyance, as I couldn't see what was so funny.

Rubble and rationing

Although the war was over, it had inflicted considerable damage on our infrastructure. The railways in particular had been subject to inordinate wear and tear and lack of maintenance. There were bombed-out buildings in most cities and towns with London and its suburbs being badly hit, but not as bad as the devastation that had been visited on places like Coventry and others, which had been singled out for their industrial importance.

Food and clothing rationing, introduced during the war to ensure people got their fair share of what was available, continued into the 1950s, and now included bread. And so began a long period of post-war austerity which lasted into the sixties.

The many bomb sites became unofficial playgrounds for children and I well remember many happy hours spent playing in the rubble of someone's home. In fact on one particular occasion I had a brush with the law whilst doing so. It happened that I had been allowed to ride my small 18-inch two-wheel bike called a 'Fairy Cycle' (I doubt you'd call it that these days!) over to my Aunt Ruby's house in Streatham to play with my older cousins, Ron and Kenny Lucas. This was basically a journey through the quiet suburban back roads and was then quite safe as there was very little traffic, few people owning cars in those days.

When I got there after about a half-hour ride, it was decided we would go for a walk up the road, where we finished up exploring one of the many bomb sites, which consisted of piles of rubble strewn with a variety of peoples belongings and abandoned household items, nothing of course of any value. On this particular site there was a large apple tree fully laden with ripe apples overhanging from an adjacent intact and occupied property. As I was the smallest my cousins suggested that they hoist me up on the garden wall so I could pick some of the apples to eat and take home.

So I was duly pushed up onto the top of the brick wall, which was about six feet high, and started to carefully pick the fruit and pass it down to Ron and Kenny. It was a slightly precarious position, so I had to concentrate and try to keep my balance while I stretched to reach the ripest fruit. While I was engrossed in my task, I vaguely remember my cousins calling out something to me, but I was concentrating too hard to take much notice. Just as I was about to turn around and pass some more fruit down, I was startled to hear a man's voice say 'And what do you think you are up to, my lad?' Terrified, I turned to see a very large policeman glaring up at me, hands on hips.

'Come on down' he ordered, and absolutely beside myself with fear, I scrambled off the wall, aided by the policeman.

'Well sonny' he said, 'Don't you know that's stealing and you could go to prison for it?' Paralysed with fear, I whimpered, 'Please sir, I only picked a very few.'

'Makes no difference,' he said. 'Where do you live?'

I grudgingly gave him my aunt's address, which he noted and

said, 'Right young lad, someone will be around to speak to your parents about this offence. Now on your way, and don't let me catch you anywhere near here again, got it?'

'Yes sir' I mumbled and duly ran back to my aunt's, where my cousins thought it was a huge joke and teased me something rotten, discussing how long I might get in prison. This frightened the life out of me until my Aunt Ruby told them to shut up and stop picking on me. She reassured me that she doubted if we'd hear any more about it as it was such a relatively trivial matter. This, of course, turned out to be the case, even though I spent a sleepless night at home worrying that at any moment there might be a knock on the door from the local constabulary.

My Auntie Ruby, of whom I was a favourite, said she wouldn't tell my mother, who would have really gone mad at me for getting into trouble. Nothing did happen of course, and after a couple of days it had gone from my mind.

However, consider if the same thing happened these days. The copper would no doubt have received a load of verbal abuse from the kids and been accused by the parents of causing trauma and mental harm!

But back then there was much more respect for authority and hence less anti-social behaviour.

Daily life in the 1940s and 50s

Day-to-day life was a something of a struggle for most families due to food shortages and clothes and furniture being invariably 'Utility' grade (a government benchmark for minimum standards) and were needless to say rather basic, although, surprise, surprise, utility furniture is now collectable!

Rationing was the norm for most items, particularly food, including sweets, and everyone had a ration book of coupons which were taken by the shop when you bought things. It was a case of 'no coupons, no sale'. These limits on the various commodities were to ensure everybody had a fair share of what was available, although the portions were quite meagre. I didn't know what a banana was until I was eight or nine! Of course inevitably a 'black market 'arose in coupons, which could be bought at a price if you knew the shady characters or crooks who dealt in them.

Life then in many ways was so very different from today. For a start, let's list the things we didn't have. Central heating was virtually unknown except in public buildings so the house was heated in winter by coal fires and hot water came from a coke boiler in the kitchen. So in the evening when sitting around the fire you tended to have your front almost singed and your back freezing from draughts!

There was no insulation in the roof or loft, and when it was really cold at night you could take an electric fire up into the bedroom while you undressed. Of course there was no such thing as an electric blanket. In the winter, I regularly awoke to find my breath giving off condensation and ice covering the inside of the window. I would leap out of bed and scuttle along to the bathroom, which was at least a little warmer due to heat from the hot water storage tank in the airing cupboard. There was no TV until the 1950s and then the sets were black and white and had tiny nine-inch screens. They took a few minutes to warm up to finally produce a rather fuzzy grey picture, primitive by today's standards.

The lady who used to do Mum's hair, Iris Curtis, a middle aged spinster, lived two roads away with her elderly parents and they were one of the very few people in the area to have a TV. Mum and I were invited round to watch the Queen's Coronation in 1952, which I remember well. To get a good view we had to sit quite close to the set, as the picture was so small, but we all thought it was wonderful.

Very few people had a telephone, although we did. Our number was Pollards 1762, which indicates how few lines there were, comparatively speaking. Mum would let neighbours in to make a call in an emergency or for family reasons, although this didn't happen very often. The phones of course were large black ebonite things with a chrome dial and instead of an area number you used the first three letters of the relevant area telephone exchange. Hence to phone us you dialled POL 1762.

I remember that on one occasion we had a call from Les' wife Aunt Nan in Sydney, Australia. About a week beforehand we were told the date and time we would get the call and to be ready to receive it, and reminded there would be a time lag on the line in view of the distance, so don't talk too fast and wait to hear the reply. When the day came mum let me listen in and I was fascinated to hear the chain of telephone exchanges along the route linking up – it was something like London-Vienna-Cairo-Johannesburg-Bombay-Singapore-Sydney – and as a result there was quite a long sound delay on the line, but at that time everyone thought it was amazing.

As an aside, at that time I was a fan of a comic book American detective, 'Dick Tracey', who had a wristwatch phone, and I remember saying to a grown- up at the time 'Won't it be great in the future when we have these?' They laughed, patted me on the head and said patronisingly 'That'll never happen!'

Of course there were no computers, internet etc, communication was only available by telephone landline at home, work or from a red telephone box and by post or telegram. There was however the radio, or 'wireless' as we called it then, which was the principal source of news and entertainment. We mainly listened to the BBC, but there was also a commercial station, Radio Luxembourg which broadcast in English with adverts. Later I discovered a US forces station based in Germany, on the short wave AFN (American

Forces Network) Stuttgart, which played a lot of jazz.

We had two wirelesses, both in polished veneered wood cases, both quite large pieces of furniture which stood on side tables and of course both were valve sets. This meant you had to turn them on and wait a couple of minutes for them to warm up. The radio was very popular and the BBC had three channels, the Home Service, the Light Programme and the Third Programme. Obviously the Light Programme was generally the most popular, having all the popular and light music and variety/comedy shows. My favourite was Childrens' Hour, which was broadcast at five o'clock and featured serials and stories, of which my favourites were Jennings at School, Norman and Henry Bones (Boy Detectives), Worzel Gummidge, Toytown and Mompty and Peckham (a cat and dog).

The radio, or wireless, was on most of the day and there were a number of good variety shows featuring musicians, singers and comedians, some of whom, like today, became celebrities with many fans. Then, of course there was the cinema or 'flics' as we called it. We had a local ABC circuit cinema, the Rex, and about a 15-minute walk away the Granada, and two or three others a short bus ride away. Dad would take Mum and me or sometimes just me on a Friday or Saturday and later I would go to the Sunday afternoon matinees. It was the heyday of films with many male and female stars who unlike today, for the most part kept their private lives discreet, which seemed to enhance their mystique and stardom.

My favourite actors and actresses were, to name a few, John Wayne, Laurel and Hardy, Jack Hawkins, Alec Guiness, Marilyn Monroe, Jane Russell and Doris Day, along with many others. A good seat cost on average about three shillings, or 15 pence in today's money. It was quite normal for there to be queues outside cinemas, especially on a Friday or Saturday night, and these were marshalled by commissionaires in smart blue or red military-style uniforms. It was all quite orderly, with normally two or three separate queues depending on the seat price. The cinemas themselves were quite stylish and ornate buildings with the interiors decorated in art deco/nouveau or ancient Egyptian style, with plush carpeting throughout.

One slightly odd aspect was that quite often people would come in midway through a film and see through the latter part first, then leave when the film came round to the point where they had come in, something you certainly wouldn't do nowadays. The typical programme would be a 'B' film first, then a break for a newsreel and adverts, then the main feature film. At the end of the last performance in the evening everyone stood for the National Anthem, with some making a quick premature dash for the exit beforehand to get to the bus stop first!

Very few people had a car – in our road of about 50 houses there were only four or five cars – so you travelled everywhere by bus, tram, trolleybus or train. Trams were phased out in the fifties and replaced by fleets of modern diesel buses, as were trolley buses, which like trams ran on electricity from an overhead gantry system but were otherwise like a normal bus. Trams ran on steel rails down the centre of the road. They have now rightfully made a comeback, especially in the Croydon area, which nowadays has an extensive network. Our local railway station, Norbury, was on the main London-Brighton line and was about a ten-minute walk away. It took about 20-25 minutes to travel to Victoria Station for the West End or London Bridge for the City.

There were no such things as supermarkets. Instead we had a whole range of shops specialising in different food and other products. Our local shops were in the High Road, part of the A23 and just ten minutes walk away. We had butchers, bakers, greengrocers, grocers, fishmongers, clothes shops, gents' outfitters. Hardware stores, haberdashers, toy shops, corn chandlers, a restaurant and a snack bar, so everyday needs were well catered for. The proprietors and staff in the shops were friendly and knew most of their regular customers.

Mother always dressed smartly when she went shopping, which was roughly every other day, and you would often meet friends and neighbours while you were out and stop for a chat, so it was a very sociable exercise.

In addition, we had deliveries from the milkman on an electric pull-along cart and the baker with a hand-pulled cart. These were daily deliveries. There was a mobile greengrocer who called weekly and a coalman once a month. The coalman, Fred Kirby, and his sons had a magnificent cart pulled by a wonderful shire carthorse. In the winter Fred had a coke brazier slung between the rear of the shafts so as 'to keep me and the horses' bums warm' as Fred put it. On cold winter days during the war Mum would give Fred a tot of whisky, which he appreciated. He would take it into the kitchen while having a chat with Mum, so shortage of coal was never a problem, even though it was rationed!

Fred adored his horse. I well remember that when his sons took over the business they decided to switch to a lorry and the horse was retired to pasture in Kent. There were tears in Fred's eyes while this tough but kind man was telling Mum this, saying how much he would miss the old 'hoss'. Indeed, there were quite a few horse-drawn carts in those days, mainly milk carts, so to see horses in the street was not at all unusual and quite often children or older ladies would come out and feed them a tit-bit like a couple of sugar cubes or a carrot.

One of the great events of the week was Sunday lunch, and Mother took great pride in her roast beef, lamb or pork, served with all the trimmings with wonderful crisp roast potatoes and two veg, usually carrots and cabbage. She would deliver this at the prescribed hour, normally half past one, and woe betide anyone late to the table, who would receive some sharp words. The dining room table was laid up on a crisply starched white damask table cloth with the best china and cutlery. No wine in those days, but the men would have a light ale to wash things down. Dad would walk down to the pub in the high road for a pre-lunch pint and chat with local friends, making sure he was back in time!

In the late 40s and 50s it would be normal for one or two of my proxy 'uncles' to be invited for lunch, and they would meet Dad in the pub. They were his friends from his pre-war bachelor days when he was in lodgings in nearby Norbury Crescent. There was Harry Swales, a large bluff Yorkshireman who worked for the Customs and Excise in London. He remained a bachelor all of his life because, as I discovered later, he suffered congenital insanity, which ran in the family. It took the form of severe depression, although he was always cheerful and good company then. Sadly I learned years later that he had committed suicide in his lodgings in Streatham.

The other 'uncle' was Fred Hemphry, who held a fairly senior position on the Southern Railway in charge of special traffic and had been instrumental in organising the trains which transported survivors from the Dunkirk evacuation around the country. He was a big portly man with a round face and he and Dad were both keen Arsenal supporters. During the war he had asked Dad if he could take Mum out now and again for a drink or the cinema, as in those days a woman would never go into a pub on her own as she would be regarded as a prostitute. Dad agreed to this, as it enabled Mum to get out for a few hours, and it was an arrangement that worked well.

I always looked forward to these lunches. It was exciting to have visitors, particularly as when they left, usually after tea with best china and a home-made sponge cake, they would discreetly present me with a silver coin, always a half-crown (12½p), a sizeable sum then. They would also always bring Mum flowers or chocolates.

Fred eventually got married, to a much younger woman who lived in Orpington, Fred's home.

Another friend from Dad's earlier days was Ted Hobday, who was also a Southern Railway man and finished up as Station Master at East Croydon, the SR's busiest station after Clapham Junction. I remember we visited him and his wife for lunch at West Malling, a station on the mainline to Dover, where he was stationmaster. As a railway enthusiast this was especially exciting for me!

Although this was a time of austerity and food money and goods in general were in short supply, I remember them as happy times. I was in a secure family, crime was low, graffiti and vandalism were relatively unheard of and people in general were well-mannered, with swearing and foul language in public frowned on very severely, so almost unheard of.

During the war my maternal grandmother lived with us. I called her 'Nan' while Mum called her 'Fan', and although in her sixties she worked sometimes six days a week at Rogers', a draper's in Streatham High Road. She was a very active old lady and could often be seen walking very briskly down our road in the mornings puffing away on a cigarette on her way to the bus stop. This was a five-minute walk away and was served by the number 133 which went to Liverpool Street Station via Streatham, Brixton, Lambeth and the City and we all used it regularly. In the late 1940s or early fifties she moved out to live with my mother's younger sister, Dorothy. I think this was because Mum said she'd done her bit looking after her and it was time one of her sisters took a turn.

Mother had two sisters, Ruby her elder sister and Dorothy, Mum being in the middle, and a brother, Leslie. She also had a half-brother, Monty. I was always curious about his origins but when I asked Mother she would brush me off, saying 'I'll tell you when you're older'.

I eventually discovered that Uncle Monty was the illegitimate son of Granny Stovold, following a liaison she had had in the 1920s. Much later I obtained a copy of Monty's birth certificate, but the details of the father are left blank. I think that at the time she might have been in service, perhaps at Eridge House, so it might have been the result of a dalliance with someone from the upper echelons of society, but this is pure conjecture and we will probably never know the truth.

Monty and Cis had a warm relationship. Aunt Cis would often refer to him as 'It" in his presence, albeit in a friendly, jovial manner, but I don't think theirs was a very passionate affair . During the war Monty had been a driver in the army, probably RASC I guess, and at one time had chauffeured George Formby, the famous Lancashire comedian and singer, while he was appearing in the ENSA shows for troops in France and Germany. After the war he had several lorry driving jobs and eventually finished up driving London buses until he retired.

My holidays with them in Devon were very happy times which I enjoyed very much.

The library

The local civic library played an important and significant part in many people's lives as membership, free to all, gave you access to the world's literature, and talks and exhibitions were held there. I was a very keen member and loved the smell of the place, a pungent aroma of floor polish and leather-bound books. My parents encouraged me to read and bought me a set of Arthur Mee's Children's Encyclopaedia, faux leather bound and quite large heavy tomes which I loved. Most evenings I was sent to bed but allowed to read until I nodded off, when someone would come and turn the light out. I was also an avid reader of the 'Biggles' books by Capt. W.E. Johns, which were stories about three Air Force pilots and their post-war adventures. It is now regarded as 'racist', but what isn't?

As a result of all this I came to love reading books, which have afforded me many hours of great pleasure and education. I now describe myself as a "bookaholic" and find it difficult to walk past a bookshop without going in.

CHAPTER 5

Country holidays

Dorothy was a lovely lady who loved nature and the countryside and was probably my favourite aunt. She had been a GPO telephonist and was married to Bert Simons, and they had a son, Peter, who is two or three years older than me. Bert was all right and I got on OK with him, but somehow I never quite warmed to him.

In my teens when Peter, who had enlisted in the Royal Navy, was away, Bert took me to classical music concerts at the Royal Festival Hall. He had had a number of jobs and for a period just after the war, during which he had been in the police force, he and Dorothy moved to the country and he worked as a farm labourer on a farm at High Easter, north Essex. I spent a couple of long school holidays staying with them in their tied cottage near the farm. It was quite an experience as there was no mains services such as water electricity and certainly no gas, so light was from oil lamps, water was pumped from a well and the radio was powered from an accumulator, a type of battery similar to a car battery.

The cottage was very old and had a thatched roof, so it was very, very rural and to me exciting, as it stood alone on a bend in the lane and was surrounded by fields and two gravel pit ponds at the rear of the cottage in a wild overgrown area which was a home to grass snakes, frogs and a variety of other wildlife. Peter and I would have great fun playing around the fields and farm and would be recruited to help in the fields at harvest time.

In particular I remember watching the reaper binder cut the hay or corn, making a circular pattern around the field which gradually got smaller and smaller so that rats and rabbits trapped in the middle would make a dash for it, chased by us lads. We also used to follow the binder and pick up the sheaves of wheat and stand them up in 'stooks' placed upright against each other in groups of five ready to be later pitch-forked up on to a cart and taken to the threshing machine. Of course this whole process nowadays is carried out much more efficiently by a combine harvester, but I'm glad I had the experience of doing it the old way. Although it was hard work it was, to me, great fun and interesting.

They moved back to London after a few years, as I think Bert was suffering back problems from the labouring. He got a job as a male telephone operator until he retired and Dorothy or 'Dot', as she was known, resumed her career, also on the exchange but not the same one as Bert.

So I have very fond memories of those days and have ever since loved living in the countryside.

Auntie Ruby

Mum's elder sister Ruby was an entirely different character. She was very fashion conscious and without doubt I was her favourite. She mas married to Ted Lucas, who was a waiter at the Dorchester so very suave and well spoken. They had two sons, Ron and Ken, again two or three years older than me – I mentioned them in my account of our brush with the law on a bomb site. They lived at 3 Downton Avenue, Streatham Hill, very near the old Streatham Hill Theatre. I used to visit them fairly regularly and Uncle Ted would take us three boys out on a Saturday or Sunday to the West End or to London Zoo or one of the great museums, which was very enjoyable.

On one particular occasion there was a discussion about where to go, and to settle the dispute Ruby suggested we should each put our choice on a piece of paper and put it in a hat for her to draw the winner. This was done and Ruby made the draw, announcing that my choice of a visit to Euston and Kings Cross Stations to see the steam trains was the winner, much to protestations of 'it's a fix!' from Kenny and hard looks from Ron. I knew that Ruby had cheated so I could see the steam engines, but kept quiet. We did the trip, much to my delight, although Kenny was a bit sulky and resentful. I did tell you I was Rubys' favourite!

Ruby had worked at the War Office during the second World War and so developed a rather posh languid upper class accent. She was a bit of a romantic and a dreamer. On one Ladies' Night at Dad's Masonic Lodge, Ruby and her partner Harry accompanied Mum and Dad to a Freemasons event at St Ermine's Hotel in Westminster. While they were having pre-dinner cocktails Ruby evidently gazed wistfully around and said 'Oh why wasn't I born to this'. Mother's comment to me on recounting this was 'silly bitch'!

Following the discovery by Ruby that Ted had had an affair with another woman, she walked out, leaving home to stay with an old family friend in Camberwell, and they were duly divorced. I remember Mum saying she was a 'silly cow' who should have swallowed her pride and got on with it, as Ted had pleaded forgiveness and promised it would never happen again. Ted Lucas eventually finished up as catering manager for Hulton Press executives, a plum job, but he was a very smooth operator and always reminded me a bit of Fred Astaire.

Ruby eventually met an accountant, Harry Steele, and years later they were married. 'Uncle' Harry was a pleasant mild-mannered man and used to drive over in his lovely Jaguar SS sports saloon and take us out on drives and picnics in the country.

However, in the meantime a furious row and ensuing feud broke out between Mother and Ruby, splitting the family for many years. What it was all about I was never quite sure. I think it centred around who would take in granny Nan in her final years, but I think there was a bit more to it than that. I would sometimes get caught in the crossfire when in my teens, particularly when on one occasion I went to a party at Ruby and Harry's in Worcester Park and arrived home more than a bit drunk. When Mother found out where I'd been she went utterly ballistic. One thing about Mother is that she had foul temper, but after she had had her say she quite quickly calmed down and didn't sulk. She hated those who did, but boy what a rage she could muster!

In the meantime Ruby had fallen out with her two sons Ron and Ken. What it was about I haven't a clue, but it got rather bitter and things came to a head when Ruby foolishly stopped sending their children birthday and Christmas presents, which as mother pointed out to her was wrong, as it wasn't anything to do with them and she would regret alienating them. Ruby, not for the first time, let her pride get the better of her and refused to back down, much, I'm sure, to her later regret.

The hatchet was finally, buried much to everyone's relief, years later after Ruby, Dorothy and Mum were widowed. On a Sunday they would all have lunch at Mum's and then I would take them all out in the country for a drive, some sightseeing and a cream tea. It was, thank heavens, now all very convivial.

However, I well remember one fateful time I agreed to take them to see the house in Reigate where they lived as children during the First World War. I eventually located the house near the railway level crossing on the outskirts of the town. Unfortunately the house was looking very run down and dilapidated and had been converted to flats. There was a rusting car on the front lawn which was overgrown and full of weeds and the large back garden they all remembered so well had been sold off for development and a row of maisonettes built. There was a sort of reflective silence in the car from them all and they were obviously sad to see the state of their old once happy home.

I thought it best to leave and off we went. On the way home they all chatted and reminisced about those old times, but I suppose its better not to go back and revisit old haunts as it invariably disappoints, in my experience.

I could never understand what all the rowing and bitterness was about, which seemed as far as I could judge very petty and trivial, and I hated the unhappiness and confrontation it created, but Mother was very bitter and sensitive about it all. There and then I resolved that I would never ever get to such a position, and if I didn't much like someone I'd just walk away or at least try and remain on polite terms with them. Such silly arguments and feuds, almost always over the most trivial incidents, are a waste of time and energy. Grow up!

After all is said and done I liked my aunts, although they were chalk and cheese –Dorothy, the country girl and Ruby, the sophisticated townie. Sadly Ruby died of dementia in a home and a couple of years later Dorothy died sitting in an armchair in her flat in Beaulah Hill, Upper Norwood, where she was found by my sister Helen, but I have fond memories of them both.

Nobby Clark

Another of Dad's friends was 'Nobby' Clarke, whose wife was 'Auntie' Nick, and they had a son, David, who was a couple of years older than me. Nobby was an official in the passport office and was a very smart, dapper man with grey hair and a moustache.

As a young man he had served in the army in the First World War, so he was a little older than the rest.

Incidentally, Dad told me once that when he was 16 he had tried to enlist in the military, the Royal Flying Corps I think, but was sent packing by the recruiting officer.

Fun on the farm

I would sometimes go round and play with David Clarke, as they lived only about 15 minutes' walk away. He was a nice lad, if a bit spoilt and wilful, but he had some great toys which I liked to play with. The Clarkes had relatives who farmed in Norfolk near a village called Kessingland, just south of Lowestoft, and one summer after the war David and I were sent up there for the summer holidays. Ivy House farm was a mixed livestock and arable farm just outside the village. I can't recall how many acres it was, but it seemed quite big to me, so I guess around 80 to 100 acres. Anyway it was great fun, and again we helped out on the farm occasionally. To reach the old stone farmhouse you drove down a quite long winding drive. In front of the house was a large muddy duckpond with an enormous weeping willow tree overhanging it, really idyllic.

The farmer, John Davey, and his wife had no children themselves but were very kind and friendly. We had the run of the whole farm, which had some lovely old buildings and barns full of old farm machinery and straw and hay. They were also infested with rats and mice, which attracted barn owls and other owls and raptors, but they were great places to explore and play.

The farm produced milk for the local area and I used to help out in the milking parlour, my main job being to run the milk through the cooler as it came fresh from the cows. It was then bottled or put in a churn for delivery. This was done using a pony-drawn milk 'float' or open-backed cart which was loaded with bottles, large necked ones with a cardboard cap, and a churn of milk. Sometimes I would go out with the milkmaid, whom I adored, a pretty 18-year-old blonde with a wonderful broad Norfolk accent. We would stop at each cottage or house and were often greeted by the owners. We either left bottles or measured out a pint from the churn and poured it into their own jug. The pony knew the round and would casually walk along, stopping where it had to without being told!

The farm also had two magnificent Suffolk Punch carthorses, gentle giants, whom we would feed and groom. There were a large number of ducks and geese roaming free and we used to go searching for their eggs around the farm, which was fun as we turned it into a competition about who collected the most.

Another favourite game was to roughly carve model boats out of soft rotting wood, add goose quills as sails and sail them on the duck pond. As the wind caught the goose quills they raced across the pond like an armada, much to our delight, and we of course organised races with them

On one memorable occasion, John Davey took delivery of the then revolutionary Ferguson tractor, which had a ground-breaking hydraulic lift on the back, making ploughing and machinery handling much easier. I well remember him showing it off to some local farmers who seemed very impressed. Climbing on to the top of a haystack with a bottle of ginger beer and lazing in the sun was bliss!

I went there twice and had such wonderful, memorable times there. I have been tempted to go back, but some years ago I happened to meet someone from Lowestoft who knew the area and said 'Don't, you won't recognise it as a lot of the farm is now a housing estate.' *Sic transit gloria mundi...*

They are very happy memories which made a great impression

on me and increased the love of the countryside and wildlife which has stayed with me throughout my life. During the war there were, of course, no holidays as such, mainly because, particularly on the south coast of England, all the beaches were closed off with barbed wire, steel scaffolding barriers and anti-tank concrete blocks, and some were mined. At key strategic points single-storey concrete 'pill boxes' were erected, manned by a handful of troops and a machine gun, the objective being to hinder and delay any German advance rather than stop it. Indeed we had specialist secret units whose role was more or less to carry out suicide attacks!

After the war things started to open up and get back to some semblance of normality. For reasons I never really knew, probably financial, after the war I went on two holidays in successive years to Devon with my Uncle Monty, Mother's half-brother and his wife, Aunt Cis. Aunt Cis was rather 'girly' and unworldly, but she was fond of me and was very good to me. Uncle Monty was very down to earth and laid back and fun to be with.

We stayed in a little village near the banks of the River Axe called, appropriately, Axmouth, which was close to the estuary and the rather larger town of Seaton. Part of the thrill for me of course was travelling down from Waterloo on a steam-hauled express train. Axmouth was an idyllic Devonshire village with a main street bordered by cottages and a church and the village pub. A small stream ran down one side of the street, so each cottage on that side had a small stone slab bridge to the front door. We stayed in one of the cottages. It was very comfortable, and the food was plain but very good. It took about 20 minutes to walk into Seaton, where there was a beach with a Fortes ice cream parlour where I was taken on the odd night as a special treat for a 'Knickerbocker Glory'.

Otherwise we would take the bus to Beer and other nearby towns like Sidmouth, and generally sightsee and paddle or splash around in the sea.

Most of the time it was just me and Aunt Cis, but Uncle Monty would come down for a few days and it was on one of his trips I decided to sail a splendid model two-masted wooden sailing boat Dad had sent me from Holland during the war. So we went down to the river, which was about 50 yards wide at this point, and launched the boat. Monty insisted that we tie a string to the back so we didn't lose it, as the wind was quite strong. Well, the string drooped in the water behind the boat and acted as a drag to stop it really sailing anywhere, so reluctantly Monty agreed to launch it without. The difference was dramatic, for the wind caught the sails and sent it off right across the estuary at a rate of knots.

Monty panicked and set off down the road to the bridge to cross to the other side of the river to try and retrieve my treasured boat. The trouble was that the shallow banks and edges of the river were very muddy, and soft mud at that, so to reach the boat, which by now had beached in the shallows, he had to go barefoot in the mud above his ankles. It was a slightly dramatic moment as Cis was in a bit of a tizzy, urging Monty to be careful and nervously wringing her hands, but all ended well with Monty drying his feet on a handkerchief and we all relaxed and had a good laugh about it.

My second and last trip to Devon was in 1949, with Aunt Cis only. It was just after receiving the news that I had passed the Eleven Plus and would therefore be going to a grammar school, much to my parents' pride and joy and to my satisfaction. I had received some coaching for it in Maths and English from a nearby lady who was a retired schoolmistress. I had rather baulked at this initially but was forced to go to, and I suppose the end justified the means. On this final trip I took my new school uniform, and I have a photo of me in it taken in Axmouth.

Subsequent holidays were spent with Mother, Father and Aunt Ruby and her then partner Harry Steele in Exmouth and Combe Martin in South and North Devon. Mother and Father and I also spent a couple of holidays in Bournemouth, where Dad in his youth had lived and sung in the local choir. He had two old school friends there and had thought of retiring there eventually, but about a year before he retired they both died, which, together with Mother's reluctance to move, made that no longer an attractive proposition. Indeed Mother's dislike of 'upping sticks' had, as already mentioned, rather adversely prejudiced Dad's career in the Bank, as if you were offered a promotion which entailed a move and didn't take it you soon became passed over fo any future opportunity. While on this subject, My sister Helen and I agree it was never a marriage made in Heaven, but rather a working partnership, as they never appeared to be very close. Helen and I have sometimes marvelled that we are here, so cool was their relationship. In fact on one occasion I heard from someone that she regarded him as a 'good catch', having a good steady pensionable job and being otherwise presentable!

I know that in the mid 1930s Mother had an affair with a man to whom I think she was very attached, but he didn't want to get married and was later killed in the war. I believe I was named after him. Also I think she had had an affair with a married man, although I'm not sure of the circumstances, except that her father was furious when he found out about it. I'm not too sure of the facts, as she would never talk much about her earlier life. The only exception to this was when she told us of her first job, which was with a mail order draper's in St Pauls Churchyard, where she worked in the despatching department.

As I have said, she had a quick temper, and thinking back I feel she harboured within her some great hurt or deep resentment which manifested itself in her temper and at times in great bitterness. She seemed at times to be at war with the world about her. But although she had a temper, she never sulked and hated those who did. She would explode with anger, but having had her say she would fairly quickly calm down.

Although Mother didn't talk much about her early life, I do remember two stories she told me. The first was about her not going to Sunday School. One Sunday afternoon two Sunday School Attendance ladies came knocking at the door and their father, who had served in the army in the First World War, answered. The rather haughty ladies said to him 'We didn't see your girls at Sunday school today, Mr Stovold'. My grandad looked at them and said 'No, and nor will you in future, don't tell me there's a God after what I've seen', at which they departed!

The second was about a costume, a skirt and jacket, which Grandad, a tailor, had made for her. The first time she wore it she was on her way out for the evening when passing the door to her father's small lounge he saw her and called her in. 'Come in, my girl, and let me have a look at you,' he said. 'Yes, it looks very well on you. If you keep your mouth shut you'll be taken for a lady!'

A new little sister

One morning in the spring of 1949, my mother said to me "Come into the kitchen, I want to talk to you". Somewhat uninterested, I sat on a kitchen chair and listened. She told me I would later that year be having a little baby brother or sister. I was a bit surprised but not at all upset at this news, which I think was to mother's relief, and life continued as normal. My sister Helen was born on 13 August 1949, while I was on holiday with Aunt Cis in Devon. On my return there was this little baby which left me, to be honest, a little bemused, mainly because the daily routine had changed quite markedly. However, I soon got used to things and was largely unaffected by the new way of life.

Helen had been born with a significant birthmark on, I think, her left eyelid, which was blue and swollen, as if she had been hit. After some consultations with doctors she was referred to Great Ormond Street Children's Hospital in London for treatment to remove the mark, which was eventually successful following treatment with radium needles and an operation. Everyone marvelled at the skill of the medics as the offending birthmark was removed without leaving a trace of a scar.

So I now had a sibling!

I do remember taking Helen out in her pram, a super de Luxe "Silver Cross", the equivalent of a Rolls Royce in the pram world, and people remarking how unusual this was as I had no inhibitions about it. The truth was that to me it was like driving a car, which was what I imagined I was doing when I took her out on the odd occasions. I particularly remember my cousin Peter Simons and me taking her out in the pram when the pavements were covered with ice and snow and playing a game, to Helen's obvious delight, of running with the pram to get speed up and the throwing on the brake so that the pram skidded along on its own for six or seven feet. This made Helen scream with laughter and delight and amused Pete and me.

However, a neighbour happened to see us doing this and told mother, who issued firm instructions that it was to stop as it was dangerous, which of course it was, as the pram could have tipped over with disastrous results.

Suffolk Punch draught horses

Wheat sheaves "stooked"

Mother in garden of no. 15, by the pond

In my new school uniform at Axemouth, 1949

On holiday with Dad - maybe Bournemouth

With Helen on her dog on wheels

Helen outside no 15, c1953

On my 'Sun Wasp' road racing bike at no. 15

My first serious girlfriend, Christine Schilling

CHAPTER 6

Schooldays

My first school was Winterbourne Road Infants, which I attended from the first September after my fifth birthday in September 1943. It was a good little school as I remember, and the Headmistress was a Miss Pegrift, a tall, smart lady who was still there when Helen went there eleven years later and remembered the Faulder name.

It was still wartime of course, although the bombing raids were far less frequent and the V1 'Doodlebugs' attacks would not begin until June 1944. I walked the mile or thereabouts to the school at first with Mother and then either on my own or with a friend and/or another parent, and walked home for lunch.

I think that it was at about the age of eight that I moved up to the junior school next door, which was boys only. I stayed there until my success in passing the Eleven Plus, which was and in some places still is the exam deciding whether you went to a grammar school or a secondary modern school.

I was quite happy there and the Headmaster, Mr J C Frame, a portly Scot, ran a tight ship, insisting on good manners and behaviour. I distinctly remember one time when the whole school was assembled to witness the public caning of three or four boys for rowdiness on their way home from school. I shudder to think what the reaction would be nowadays to such action. However it certainly enforced good behaviour and I don't think the lads in question suffered any PTSD!

One boy my age, Kenny, lived on the corner of our road and suffered badly with asthma, so I would sometimes accompany him to and from school in case he had a problem with his breathing, when I could get help. So far as I know he was one of very few children in the school who had a persistent health problem, as compared with nowadays when so many young people have a whole range of debilitating or potentially lethal health issues from asthma through a range of allergies. What has happened to cause this?

Much to my and my parents' delight I passed the written Eleven Plus, for which I received some coaching from a local retired lady school teacher. I had to attend an interview with a panel of heads or deputy heads of the local grammar schools, of which there were four, John Ruskin, Selhurst, Archbishop Tennysons, and Whitgift. We all gathered at a local school and waited nervously to be called in groups of six or seven to be interviewed by the panel. I don't remember much about it except one boy, who when asked what his ambition was said 'to be an undertaker'. This raised a faint smile on the faces of the panel, as they correctly assumed he meant underwriter.

I received a letter some days later to confirm I had been selected to attend John Ruskin Grammar School in Croydon, a 20-minute bus ride away to West Croydon plus a short walk. I started there in September 1949. My father had been concerned about the choice of school as he had heard that Ruskin had been something of a socialist. However on further investigation this proved to be rather overstated, and in any case all schools were strictly forbidden to pursue any kind of political agenda, so that was that.

The first day was a bit daunting with getting used to the new surroundings and the school routine along with a host of new masters, but it was well organised and all of us in the new intake quickly settled in. As first formers we were called 'Brats' by the older boys and regarded as the lowest of the low, but there was very little if any bullying, so we all accepted it and got on with life. It was an all boys' school, as was the norm then, and the teaching staff were all male except for one quite feisty middle-aged lady, and discipline was firm but not oppressive. We all called the masters 'Sir' and stood up when they entered the room at the start of each lesson. I quickly made a number of friends and my memories of the time I spent there are very good. However discipline was fairly strict and the use of corporal punishment was deemed quite acceptable to reinforce it.

I do well remember an incident in my third year there which happened during an English Literature lesson given by our English master, Mr Griffiths. During the course of the lesson I made a paper dart, but was caught in the act of throwing it across the classroom. This earned me a hard slap around the head which almost knocked me out of my desk and a detention during which I had to write out 200 times 'Aeronautics is the science of flight', which I have never forgotten. But again I suffered no PTSD! Heaven knows what the reaction would have been today.

Each day started with an assembly in the main hall where there were prayers and a hymn followed by announcements by the Head or Deputy Head concerning events, admin and the like, terminated by reciting the Lord's Prayer. Of course at that time there were no Muslims, Hindus and the like, with only two Jewish boys, who were allowed to abstain from the religious bits.

After a while, if the weather was dry, I would cycle to and from school, although then the traffic was much lighter, so not so hazardous by a long way as compared to today.

The school had an Army Cadet Unit, which I joined, and we paraded after school on a Friday. We did drill, including arms drill with old First World War rifles, no ammunition of course, and generally did standard infantry training including fieldcraft and platoon attacks – great fun! We were 'J' Company, Cadet Battalion, The Queen's Royal Regiment and proud of it. Sometimes we would go down to the local Territorial Army indoor rifle range and practise shooting with .22 rifles, which we all loved to do, but of course we were strictly supervised. We also went on summer camps which were under canvas at Shorncliffe near Folkstone, usually for a week, when we trained at the various military skills and did 'Exercises' involving military manoeuvres etc.

We were all encouraged to take the Army proficiency exam 'Certificate A', which I did, and this entitled you to wear a red star badge on your tunic sleeve, which I did with some pride. Bear in mind that I was then due to do National Service in the armed forces for two years when I was eighteen, so I was reasonably well prepared. On our Friday afternoon parades we would regularly receive instruction from a regular army NCO, usually a sergeant, who would give instruction on infantry tactics, weapon training, map reading and foot drill. The foot drill could be quite awesome, as it was usually done by a Brigade of Guards sergeant who presented an impressive sight in his immaculate khaki uniform with his stern no-nonsense attitude. They were sticklers for discipline and we were very much in awe of them. When they said 'jump' you said 'how high?'!

When I first attended JRGS it was in Tamworth Road in a classic turn of the century school building complete with a bell tower. Later, in my fourth year, it was moved into modern, custom-built premises in Shirley Hills on the outskirts of Croydon and within walking distance of the Shirley Hills open common. It was built in the grounds of a windmill which had been renovated and was very well equipped with science labs, library, sports facilities and gymnasium etc. It was much further out, thus a longer bus ride, but within reasonable cycling distance, so in fine weather I would often cycle there. There's a photo of me with Mike Pike and two other boys during a lunchtime bowling session in the cricket nets.

I discover Jazz

It was during my latter days at Grammar school that I discovered jazz. I can't quite recall now how it all came about, but my pals and I became great fans of what was then known as 'Traditional Jazz". At that time Chris Barber and his band had broken into the Hit Parade with a jazz version of 'Bobby Shafto' which proved very popular. We all started collections of the 78rpm shellac record discs which were then the norm for recording, although of course they were very brittle and could easily be cracked or broken, so they were handled with care. They had a playing time of about three minutes, which was just about adequate for most pop songs. Eventually, in the sixties, vinyl records, much more durable and with longer playing time, arrived.

At this time we heard there was a jazz club every Friday night at the 'Star' pub at Broad Green, West Croydon, so we all agreed to meet there, and it became a regular haunt. The resident band was Mike Daniels' Delta Jazz Men, who were a very professional and polished jazz group, and we had some wonderful nights there. It was also there that I met Bob Pearse and Tony Crotty, who would become good friends.

After a while I really fancied taking up an instrument and chose what was then my favourite, the clarinet. There was some opposition to this at home as it was felt that it would be a 'nine-day wonder' and thus a waste of money as a halfway decent second hand clarinet cost around £25! Peanuts by today's standards, but more than a month's wages then for most people. As I wasn't working it would be my parents who would foot the bill and they were needless to say very reluctant about the whole thing.

Then enter Aunt Nell. She wasn't really a blood aunt but a long standing family friend from their days in Brixton. She was, I think, a Jewish lady and a great character. Only 5' 2" or so, she was the life and soul of any party. I remember her at one family Christmas do tucking her skirt in her knickers and doing a tap dance. She was also an accomplished pianist and had regularly played in cinemas accompanying silent films.

Anyway she happened to pay us a visit around this time and seeing I was very 'down' about not being able to have a clarinet, she had a quiet word with my parents, persuading them to indulge me. Good old aunt Nell! Thus a week later I was making squeaks and honks on my first musical instrument. To my parents' surprise, I stuck with it and got myself some lessons with Jack Bonsor, then the lead saxophone with the famous Sydney Lipton society orchestra in the West End. Eventually I took up the alto saxophone as well, but that's another story!

In those days, as a young boy, anywhere you went you would go on your bike, so bikes became a bit of a status symbol and a great deal of pride was taken in maintaining them and making sure you had a 'good spec' so far as equipment such as brakes, gear systems, lights, tyres, wheels etc were concerned.

Quite often you would go out to some local park or similar venue to hang out with your pals, and this included girls. They were especially impressed (or at least said they were) by a young blade with a flashy bike, and the boys would show off blatantly to try and impress the girls by staging races or time trials around the roads. Of course, inevitably your clothes, although nothing special by today's standards but nevertheless a smart shirt, pullover and trousers, were good for the image.

When I was about 15, my cousin Ronnie enlisted into the Parachute Regiment. Now Ron had a superb 'Sun Wasp' bike, a road racing model with a really fantastic spec. It had a yellow frame with chromed forks front and rear and a superb French 'Simplex' gear system, and the whole thing was as light as a feather. My parents were persuaded to buy this from Ron for not very much, maybe £20 or so, which put me in pole position with my pals, especially the girls, and coupled with the fact that I sported a gaberdine windcheater covered with the embroidered cloth shields, sewn on by my mother, of the various Swiss cantons and towns I had visited on a school trip. Well, I was really fancying my chances!

It was then and there that I met my very first girlfriend, Christine Shilling, a lovely brunette, dark and slim with brown eyes and flawless complexion. I quickly became besotted with her and she with me, and our relationship flourished until after my demob from the army. We regularly wrote to each other and I well remember my reaction when I first saw her on my return from Malaya – WOW, what a looker! Chris had developed into a beautiful young woman and we continued our romance for some months. However, she was eager to settle down, get married and start a family, but simply, I was not so inclined. Gradually our relationship started to become distant and eventually Chris said she didn't want to carry on and had met someone else.

It is true to say I was devastated, although it was entirely my fault, thinking that she would always be around ready for the time I felt like getting married. In spite of my pleadings she was adamant, which left me very upset for some months. I have often wondered how it might have worked out for us had we married, as many years later I heard that she had had a very unhappy first marriage and had a handicapped child by her second husband. In view of my subsequent poor marital track record of three failed marriages, would it have been the same, or was this unhappy relationship with Chris the root cause of the later instability in my life? I must stress that I hold myself entirely to blame for all past failures in wedded bliss, and no one else. But I wonder.

Grammar school

Much has been written about the Eleven Plus exam and grammar schools and how socially divisive they were. Well, that wasn't my experience, as I had many friends who went to the local secondary modern schools, as they were called and there was certainly never a hint of 'them and us' – in fact we seldom if ever discussed our schooling. Many of these friends went on to have successful careers in well-paid jobs, and conversely some of my grammar school contemporaries went into some quite low level, mundane occupations. The system did sift out the more academically inclined, but even then not too many went on to university, which was then the exception rather than the rule. I am firmly of the opinion that the idea that you are not properly educated unless you've been to university is quite wrong and wholly misguided. In my opinion there are nowadays too many second rate 'universities' or so called, which are little more than colleges of further education with a new brand name peddling spurious degrees in order to get bums on seats to increase their income.

A large number of those who do go through the university system, in my experience, come out with a huge debt and no more breadth of knowledge or cultural experience than when they started. Far better to go to a technical college or serve an apprenticeship to learn a trade or skill. My own experience reflects this. I went into the sixth form to take 'A' Level exams having gained a basic but undistinguished number of 'O' Levels in Mathematics, English

Literature, English Language and Geography. However I was, I suppose, a bit half-hearted about the end goal, which might, a very big might, have been university, placing an expensive burden on my parents which would have been a stretch for them.

CHAPTER 7

Starting work

Many of my friends and contemporaries had left school and were in jobs earning money and becoming more independent, which appealed to me more at the time. Also compulsory National Service for two years in the armed forces loomed when I was seventeen and a half. So after a talk with my parents it was agreed that I would leave school when I had found a suitable job, which would probably be in the 'City'.

So I began to search the two London evening newspapers, the *Evening Standard* and the *Evening News*, both of which advertised extensive numbers of jobs in the 'Situations Vacant' columns. It's strange to think that then there was no shortage of work as the papers were full of all sorts of jobs listed in columns on maybe two or three pages. There were large numbers of vacancies in the banking, insurance and shipping sectors in particular. Britain had a large number of passenger and cargo shipping lines, which is not surprising as most intercontinental travel was by sea until maybe the late 1960s, when cheap affordable air travel started to become available. This eventually led to the demise of many of the old shipping companies or their move into the cruise market. My plan, which I worked out with my father, was to get a job which would be pensionable and see how it worked out. Employers were obliged by law to hold a position open for you on your demob from National Service, so job security was not a problem. I would consider what next on my return.

As it turned out I liked the job I had selected, more or less at random, with a company of Lloyds' Insurance Brokers and this ultimately developed into a successful career for me. My parents were very concerned that I should get a secure pensionable job and their obsession with security is understandable if you consider their lives to date. They had been born just before the First World War, then reached maturity during the great financial depression of the late twenties and early thirties and married and started a family just in time for World War 2!

A career in the city

Almost the first job I applied for was with a Lloyds' insurance broker, Bland, Welch & Co, who required a junior assistant in their Marine Claims department. So, wearing a new £10 suit from Burtons, I attended my first interview at St Mary at Hill just off Billingsgate Market, where I was ushered into the office of the company's staff officer, Mr Stacey-Salmon (known, I afterwards discovered, as 'Fish'). He was a very pleasant man and soon put a rather apprehensive me at ease and we had a good chat. I thought it had gone well, which proved the case as I was shortly after summoned back for a second interview with my boss to be, the Marine Claims director, Mr N K Payne. He was a physically big man who had been a Cambridge Blue at Rugby, but quiet in manner and a strong presence. Again I thought I had acquitted myself well and to my great pleasure a few days later I received a job offer at £225 a year salary pensionable after a year and a two shillings and sixpence (12½p) luncheon voucher every day. Luncheon Vouchers were then very much the thing and were exchangeable at most city restaurants and eateries, where it would more or less on average get you a decent two-course meal, eg sausage and mash followed by jam roly poly.

Lloyds

So began my career in the 'City'. My first job was to act as a sort of messenger boy-cum-postman delivering marine Hull and Cargo claims documents to the various companies and to Lloyds' Underwriters, which entailed going into Lloyds' Underwriting Room early in the morning to collect the numerous claims documents, check they had been approved and deliver them to the next underwriter on the list for similar approval. I also had to answer, or obtain answers to, any queries which might have arisen. To explain this a little, each risk or insurance was underwritten or insured by a number of both Lloyds' and company underwriters on a percentage basis, thus spreading the risk, so in the event of a claim each one had to approve settlement. There were of course short cuts to this otherwise tedious operation, but I won't bore you with that!

I well remember my first introduction to the Underwriting Room at Lloyds'. It was like entering another world and would play a major part in the rest of my working life. This vast open marble-clad arena, for the want of a better word, was a hive of bustling activity with the scarlet-coated 'waiters' or attendants and the rostrum topped by the Lutine Bell, all engaged in insuring the world's shipping and major industrial companies. It was at the same time awesome and exciting to me. Here I was working at the coalface of one of the world's most important financial institutions.

Gradually, as I got the hang of things, I became more knowledgeable and started to help my senior claims clerks with the preparation process, thus serving a sort of apprenticeship, and was gradually able to take a more responsible role. I remember using a mechanical calculator which enabled you to do mathematical sums by adjusting levers and turning a handle, crude by today's standards but effective nonetheless. I enjoyed the job, as it meant I wasn't deskbound but had the freedom to roam the city and Lloyds' almost at will, providing the job was done. Fine when it wasn't raining!

Our offices were at 9-10 St Mary at Hill, and just opposite was a small Italian run restaurant which served a variety of English as well as Italian fare at a cost of around three shillings or so, plus a tip of a few coins. I palled up with a couple of men from the nearby wine importers and a couple of colleagues, so lunch was quite a pleasant social affair.

CHAPTER 8

National Service

All was going well – and then came my call-up papers from the government for National Service. I was summoned for a medical and interview at the recruiting office in West Croydon, which I duly attended. I was tipped off by my school friends not to mention my Army Cadet training, as this would very likely cause me to be put in the Guards or an infantry regiment, where the chances of going abroad were hit or miss, and I desperately wanted to serve abroad, preferably in a warm climate! Bear in mind that at that time Britain had bases all over the globe: Germany, Cyprus, North Africa, Aden, Singapore and Malaya, Christmas Island, Malta, etc.

I passed the medical as expected and awaited my call-up papers for my two years' service. After a couple of weeks my enlistment papers came through and I was ordered to report to Blackdown Camp, on the Hampshire/Surrey border, a training facility for the Royal Army Ordnance Corps, whose role was to keep the army supplied with arms, ammunition and equipment. I was quite pleased at this as army units, wherever they were, needed this logistical support, so the chances of an overseas posting were much greater than if I had been sent to an infantry regiment.

So on 7th February 1957, with a rail warrant and a small case with my toilet kit and a few odds and ends, I said goodbye to my parents and took the train to Waterloo Station, where I would get another to Brookwood on the Surrey-Hampshire border for Blackdown Camp. When I reached the platform at Waterloo it was packed with young men my age, all obviously bound for the same or similar camps. We all tried to look nonchalant and relaxed, but we were really more than a little apprehensive.

We climbed aboard the train, more or less keeping ourselves to ourselves, and clattered along for about forty minutes or so until it finally came to a halt at Brookwood Station, where army lorries were waiting to take us to Blackdown Camp.

Our arrival at Brookwood was a rather sombre, even macabre, affair, as the place is famous for having one of the largest cemeteries in the country and is known as a 'necropolis'. It was laid out in Victorian times to cater especially for the dead from London, where local churchyards in and around the capital were overflowing; cremation didn't take off until the early 20th century. In the cemetery's heyday regular funeral or 'coffin' trains ran from Waterloo to Brookwood, transporting the deceased to their final resting places, where they were interred with all due rites as if being buried in their local churchyard. This huge cemetery partly borders the railway line at Brookwood and as you look out of the train window or from the platform, all you can see is acres of tombstones and accompanying statuary. As I say, a sobering sight!

Army days

We were all packed into an army lorry standing up and hanging on as we bounced along the country roads to Blackdown Camp. On arrival we were organised into groups or platoons of about 20 and 'processed', which meant being marched around to collect our army issue clothing, uniforms, mess kit and bedding, which were deposited in our barrack block, a two-storey building with communal wash basins and toilets. Our hair was cut at the regimental barber shop to a very 'short back and sides' and I remember the dismay and moans from some of the 'Teds' or Teddy boys' at losing their Tony Curtis hairstyles. The 'Teds' were a cult of the 1950s, so named after the Edwardian-style dress they wore of drainpipe trousers, drape jackets, bootlace ties and the like. Rock 'n roll was their music.

We were there to undergo six weeks' basic training, which covered drill, infantry tactics, route marches, rifle drill and shooting interspersed with physical training. Every morning there was a kit inspection, which entailed laying out your kit on the bed in a prescribed fashion and blankets 'boxed', i.e. folded neatly into an oblong shape with the over blanket wrapped around them. We then 'stood by our beds' at attention until the kit had been inspected by the orderly officer and sergeant. Woe betide anyone with dirty or scruffy kit – they would be admonished severely and often put on a charge, resulting mainly in being placed on 'fatigues' such as 'spud bashing' (potato peeling) or cleaning. We also had to do guard duty, which consisted of a spit and polish parade of the guard contingent in the late afternoon, then off to the guardhouse, where the guard commander, usually a sergeant, allocated you your shift or 'stag' as it was known. This was four hours on and four hours off, so depending on the number on guard and the different areas to be patrolled it could mean two stags of four hours, then up and ready at 6 am to continue training! I well remember wandering around my patrol area in late February starting at 2 am until 6 with a hard frost coming down, armed with a pick handle, half awake and bloody cold and bored!

Another chore was so called 'bulling' your boots, which was to polish the toe caps and heels of your best boots so that they shone like mirrors. Now this was long and tedious work, as the boots were issued with pimpled leather caps and heels and you had to bone them with a piece of bone, or, more normally, a toothbrush handle or spoon handle and a lighted candle to heat the polish so that it formed a hard glossy surface on the boots. It took hours and was tedious work, but the end result was somehow very satisfying when you had done it and your boots gleamed. Of course, once you had achieved this happy state you were very careful to protect them and try not to get them scratched. These best boots were then reserved for special parades, as you also had a pair of 'working' boots for everyday use which still had to be polished but not 'bulled up'.

Our immediate superior was a muscular, blond 'Geordie' corporal who was tough but very fair and in a way acted not only as our instructor and disciplinarian but also almost as a father figure to us. I gather he had been in the ill-fated parachute assault on Arnhem, so he had seen serious action and thus received great respect.

Finally, after six weeks or so, we completed our basic training and were ready to 'pass out', with everyone parading together in a ritual ceremony to mark our becoming trained soldiers. In the lead up to this there was a competition to assess the smartest recruit in dress, drill and ability, who would receive an award. I was short-listed for this and ended as runner up, which I was quite pleased with. Our parents, wives etc were invited to come and witness this parade, and my parents did. It was quite a spectacle, with a military band leading the march past. Afterwards I went home with them for a week or so's leave to await posting to a Trade Training School.

In the RAOC there were a number of trades relating to its role as equipment, ammunition and arms supplier to the army at large; these were Storeman, Ammunition Examiner, Driver, and Clerk Technical or Clerk General Duties. I was eventually posted for training as a Clerk Tech or GD back to Blackdown, but in a different part of this very big camp. The discipline was much more relaxed and our instructor was a genial young man not much older than us who laboriously took us through all the different army forms and procedures for about a fortnight. We then took a written exam to test our knowledge and were advised that those who made the best marks would get the best overseas postings.

I was now desperate to get an overseas posting to somewhere hot like Cyprus or the Far East, so I swotted hard with my comrades. This proved very fruitful as I achieved a mark of just over 90%! Thus I looked forward with bated breath to find out where I would be going.

After a day or so we were told the postings were up on a noticeboard outside the Company Office and we hurried over there to discover our future. With some trepidation I scanned the noticeboard until I saw 23371145 Pte Faulder G... Singapore! I was absolutely ecstatic, for this was the one posting I had longed for and I could hardly believe my luck. So I packed up all my kit and went off on embarkation leave for a fortnight.

My parents were also, I think, pleased with my news, my father saying that it would be good for me and that 'travel broadens the mind'. My mother was a little concerned that I might be led astray by the wiles of some dusky Asian or slinky Chinese female. Needless to say, I was not!

So with some 'stiff upper lip' goodbyes I slung my kitbag on my shoulder and set off to the station to get the trains back to Blackdown to be kitted out and transported to Southampton Docks to board the ship for Singapore. I wouldn't see home again for nearly two years.

Back at Blackdown I met up with some of my new pals and was issued with tropical kit, and finally the great day arrived. Just before this the sergeant in charge of us asked for two volunteers to form an advance party to escort some of the general stores on board and prepare the ship for the main group's embarkation.

Now in the army the golden rule is 'never volunteer', but so keen was I to get going I shot my hand up immediately, as did another of my new mates, Tommy Mclean, a Scot from Dumbarton with a very broad accent. We were duly appointed as the advance party, which proved to be a very lucky break.

The following day we climbed into an army lorry with the stuff we were escorting and trundled off to Southampton.

Sailing the ocean blue

We arrived at the docks and came to a stop alongside a large white ship, the TT *Dunera*, a former Bibby Line passenger ship converted as a troop transport. Bear in mind that at that time, with all the British overseas bases, it required a fleet of such vessels to fetch and carry the military personnel, both Army and Air Force (the Navy for obvious reasons didn't need it). As we got aboard we were met by the ships RSM (Regimental Sergeant Major), who asked us what our educational qualifications were. This seemed a bit odd, but when we answered with our GCE passes in English and Maths, he seemed impressed and said he wanted us to man the ship's orderly room, which was the admin office for the troops while they were on board. We both accepted with alacrity as it meant we wouldn't be below decks with the main body of men with their inevitable BO and smelly socks, but on the weather deck. Also with our Orderly Room armbands we had the run of the ship, including the NCOs' and Officers' quarters. Quite a coup, we thought, and so it turned out to be.

We didn't have a below deck berth like the other troops but slept on stretchers in the Orderly Room, and this was an arrangement that worked well. We didn't have that much to do, our main tasks being to type up Daily Standing Orders and run off duplicate copies on a Banda duplicating machine. This meant placing a special waxed paper in the typewriter, typing the orders onto it, then taking the wax 'skin' and clipping it onto a drum which you turned by hand. As the drum rolled around it was inked and impressed onto the paper to reproduce the text on the skin. Primitive by today's standards but it worked. Other than that we dealt with general enquiries and were 'gofers' taking messages to various people around the ship, quite a cushy number really.

Now this was at the time just after the Suez crisis and as a result the Suez Canal was closed, so we had to go the long way around Africa and the Cape of Good Hope We duly set sail and all went well for a few hours until we sailed into the notorious Bay of Biscay and into a storm. Now the *Dunera* was a bit of an old tub and she pitched and rolled in the storm like a bucking bronco. To move around the ship you had to grab anything firm and stagger along from rail to rail or whatever was handy. Every so often the bows would rear up into the air then crash down with a shuddering force, so that the propellors at the stern came out of the water and raced, making the whole ship vibrate. Needless to say almost everyone was seasick as a result and there was vomit everywhere, not just in the toilets.

To cap it all, when we staggered down to the mess for breakfast on the first morning the meal was kippers and an orange! Very few takers, as you can imagine. I lasted out until then but eventually succumbed for a few hours. So not a very auspicious start to our voyage. However 24 hours later the next day the sun was out and we sailed peacefully along in calmer waters off the coast of Portugal.

I think it was on about the third day that George, the ship's Purser, came to see us in a very agitated state as his duplicator had broken and he was unable to print the menu for the officers and their ladies in first class. Now George was, looking back, gay, but he was a decent man and very worried that the Captain would be very upset with him if there were no menus. We readily agreed to type and print the menus for him, and he was very visibly relieved and said he would see us right for getting him out of a mess. Sure enough he was as good as his word and kept us supplied throughout the voyage with 'posh nosh' from the first class menu as well as beer and scotch.

We all very quickly settled into the ship's routine, which included PT and shooting at floats, although as Orderly Room staff we were excused most of this and the ship's RSM, our boss, left us pretty much to our own devices providing everything ran smoothly, which we made sure it did. He took us both aside on one occasion and told us confidentially that if he was required in an emergency and was not in his cabin, we should knock discreetly on such and such a cabin in the female quarters! We of course agreed and, more importantly, we would forget these instructions unless there was a real emergency. It was obvious that he was having a relationship with a WRAC (Women's Royal Army Corps).

Africa, Mauritius and Ceylon (Sri Lanka)

We were now sailing down the West African Coast towards our first port of call, Dakar in Senegal, and a few days later we docked there in the blazing hot sun. We were all given a few hours' shore leave to have a look around Dakar, which was a very run down former French colonial city with few metalled roads. My only real memory of it was going into a public toilet and being confronted with the most appalling stench and a stand-up toilet with foot positions on a dirty ceramic base. I immediately lit up two 'Lucky Strikes' to combat the smell! Back on board we continued our journey down the coast of West Africa with the next port of call being Cape Town, a much better prospect to explore. And so it proved, a beautiful city sheltering under the imposing backdrop of Table Mountain.

A group of us set out to explore the city, but the first thing we noticed was the profusion of notices saying, sometimes in Afrikaans, 'Whites Only' or 'No Blacks', for this was the height of the Apartheid era. All was going well until we stopped to talk to a young black kid on a bike delivering newspapers. We were chatting to him about nothing very much, certainly nothing political, when suddenly two white SA policemen roared up on motorcycles and addressed us aggressively, saying 'Who are you and why are you speaking to this person? You don't talk with them at all, see!' We were all somewhat taken aback at this, especially when they said 'We could arrest you for this'.

This really got up my nose and I turned and said to them, 'We are guests of the Mayor of Cape Town and are not familiar with your laws here'. Although technically true, this was stretching things a bit. Also, we were all in uniform. This fazed them a bit and they looked at each other then said 'OK, but you don't talk to these people' and roared off, having sent the young black lad away with a warning to him to stay away from us.

So, that was my first experience of Apartheid. I felt it to be all rather sinister and threatening, even though I was white.

We rejoined the ship later that afternoon after a short visit to the relatively nearby beach for an hour or so, which was a pleasant interlude.

As the sun was setting, with us all lining the ship's rail and to the sound of the famous lady in white standing on the pier head singing 'Now is the hour', we were reversed out of the harbour by tugs, passing a number of British Union Castle Line ships berthed in the docks on the way, which was quite a sight and not a little emotional. Bear in mind that these were the days before long distance air travel became the norm and most long journeys were by sea, so the UK in particular had a large merchant marine fleet with a number of different shipping lines, each with a sizeable fleet of passenger or cargo ships.

As we were doing this there was a disturbance of some kind further along the deck with a lot of shouting and a bit of a tussle between a few people. It turned out later that this had been caused by a young soldier whose girlfriend had sent him a 'Dear John' letter, as they were known, ending their relationship, which had made him try to jump overboard.

So we started the next leg of our journey, which was to Port Louis, Mauritius, a beautiful island in the Indian Ocean, another picturesque former French possession in an idyllic setting. We were unable to tie up at the dockside as the water was too shallow, so we anchored just outside the main dock area and were ferried ashore by barges. As we clambered up onto the landing stage there was a crowd of locals waiting to try to sell a variety of items, souvenirs and the like.

After a wander around Port Louis, a fine old French Colonial port town, half a dozen of us were invited to a beach party a short drive away. This was from the RAF, who had a communications centre on the island. We drove in a Land Rover up and along winding roads, mostly dirt, through sugar cane plantations until we came to a fantastic beach. It had silver sand and swaying palms with the ocean lapping gently against the shore, protected by a large coral reef about fifty yards out. We were supplied with a simple picnic lunch and some beer and spent a wonderful few hours lazing in the tropical sun with the occasional splash about in the sea. All the time we were there, an old native in a sort of dug-out boat was paddling up and down just inside the reef, gazing about him all the while. When the RAF driver came to pick us up, I commented to him that the old guy fishing didn't seem to have caught much. He looked at me and grinned, 'He wasn't fishing mate, he's the shark lookout!' 'Blimey!' I said.

And so we went back on board. As we gently weighed anchor and sailed slowly back out to sea past the palm-fringed shore in the setting sun, I vowed to return someday, so captivated was I by the place. Many years later I did return and wasn't disappointed, for it was every bit as beautiful and magical as I remembered.

Our next port of call was to be Colombo, the capital of Ceylon (now Sri Lanka). This entailed a cruise across the Indian Ocean and it became very hot. Tommy Mclean and I were very glad we were on the upper weather deck, which was much cooler at night, rather than in the troop decks, where there was limited ventilation and certainly no air conditioning. This was particularly preferable at night when we slept on our stretchers with a cool breeze wafting through the Orderly room, making it much more comfortable.

One morning, another warm bright sunny one, the cry went up 'Dolphins!' so I rushed up to the open deck, but in so doing I cracked my head while jumping over the raised ridge on the doorway threshold, It hurt, certainly, but I kept going to the rail as far forward as I could get to hang over it and wonder at the sight of a school of twenty-plus dolphins riding the bow wave of the ship and leaping out of the water, then diving under the bows to reappear some yards ahead. This was a wonderful sight and they were so obviously just playing and showing off their amazing aquatic skills. I have never tired of watching these wonderful, graceful creatures. Flying fish also regularly scudded around the ship.

By now my injury was bleeding somewhat and I was holding a handkerchief on top of my head to stem the blood. After a while went to the ship's medical centre to have it looked at, but it was only a relatively minor injury, so I was given a plaster and sent on my way.

One hot sultry evening during the voyage across to Colombo, George, the Purser, came up for a chat and brought us a few bottles of beer. As they were a bit warm, Tam and I decided one way to cool them would be to put them in a bag and lower them into the water through a porthole, which we proceeded to do. We left them for about half an hour before hauling them up, but when we opened the bag all that was there was a lot of broken glass! We had overlooked the fact that the ship was travelling at around 12 knots and gently rolling. We had got so used to it that we didn't feel it. Each time she rolled, the bag on our rope went out about 3 or 4 feet from the side of the ship and then, as the ship rolled the other way, it came crashing back against the steel hull, with the inevitable result. We philosophically laughed it off and chalked it up to experience.

During this leg of the voyage the Entertainments Officer decided it would be a good idea to organise a concert for the troops with acts recruited from passengers of all ranks. This should relieve the boredom that was setting in and would be good for morale. It was to take place in the troops' saloon bar area, which was quite large, and a makeshift stage was erected. It became a sort of early version of 'Britain's Got Talent', as it turned out. Our boss, the ship's RSM, was a bit dubious about the idea, especially when it was discovered that a couple of officers' wives would be taking part.

The concert started one afternoon about an hour after the troops were assembled en masse in the saloon. They were busy knocking back pints, with the inevitable result that by the time the concert started most squaddies were getting pretty well oiled. The various amateur acts were generally treated with good humoured derision and barracked a bit but generally well received, the earlier acts being from the troop deck. Then the time came for the finale, which consisted of two officers' wives singing songs from Gilbert and Sullivan and other light music composers. By this time the whole troop deck was in a raucous, drunken state, having been wound up by a couple of their number miming to Bill Haley's

'Rock around the Clock', which ended in thunderous applause and cheering etc.

Then the MC, a sergeant, got up and announced that an officer's wife, Mrs So and So, would like to sing some popular songs for them. This very attractive lady got up on the stage in an evening gown to polite applause and announced that her first number would be Ivor Novello's 'We'll Gather Lilacs'. This was very much at the other end of the spectrum from Bill Haley and the rock n' rollers! There was silence, then the pianist started an introduction and the lady launched into a very creditable performance of the number – she had quite a good voice, but the performance was received in deathly silence by the very well sauced men in the audience. When she finished there was a brief eerie silence, then suddenly the place erupted with thunderous cheering and a standing ovation, much to the amazement of the lady artiste. This was followed by shouts of 'More, more!'

The few senior NCOs and officers who had discreetly crept in to the back of the room were as astonished as the rest of us onlookers. Later, the officer whose wife it had been buttonholed me and said 'I understand, Faulder, that the men very much enjoyed my wife's performance yesterday.'

'Yes sir, they certainly did,' I replied, 'but it was also partly because they appreciated that she took the trouble to make an effort to entertain them and they admired her courage.'

'Well well,' he said, shaking his head.

I thought it wise not to mention that the sight of an attractive woman in an evening gown displaying, albeit tastefully, a very good figure, was manna from heaven to a bunch of virile young men deprived of female company. Indeed later that day I well remember a Scot from one of the Highland Regiments saying 'Ay, she was a braw lassie and she had some balls!'

A few uneventful days later we arrived at Colombo and were

ferried ashore on some sizeable barges As we clambered up onto the quayside, a crowd of locals were waiting for us and immediately accosted us with all manner of gifts, mostly cheap rubbish. As I pushed my way through the throng I was approached by a young lad pushing a bike who thrust a scrappy piece of paper in front of me on which was scrawled 'You like my sister, she as clean and white as Queen Victoria'. I shook my head and declined his kind invitation.

I don't recall much about Colombo itself but nevertheless felt a thrill and exultation about finally being in the one of the exotic places my seafaring uncles had talked about.

After a few hours ashore, it was back on board to begin the final leg of our journey down the Straits of Malacca to Singapore.

Singapore

The voyage down the Malacca Straits was uneventful, and eventually after about a month at sea we arrived at Singapore. We slowly navigated through the 'roads' or shipping lanes and moorings until we were nudged into our berth by the tugs, amid much shouting by the Chinese tug crews. My first comment was 'Christ, it's hot and sticky' mixed with some awe and excitement as at that time I had no idea which particular unit I had been posted to.

After a seemingly endless wait at the top of the gangplanks we finally staggered off with all our kit and were ordered into army lorries to take us to our various locations. My truck rattled through the streets of Singapore until it reached the vast army transit camp at Nee Soon. There, a sergeant gave us our posted unit, and mine turned out to be 21 Air Maintenance Platoon, Kuala Lumpur, Malaya. This would entail an overnight rail journey up country, so I was told to go to the mess for a meal and then report in the late afternoon to the Armoury to be issued with a rifle and ammunition and transport to the railway station.

When I queried why I needed a rifle I was told "You will be on guard for part of the journey as the train has in the past been ambushed by CTs (Communist Terrorists)" I didn't feel too concerned about this, but was very excited as I contemplated the adventure I was about to embark on.

Off I went to the mess and got some food from the servery. I looked around for an empty seat but the place was quite full. Eventually I saw a spare seat on the end of a table full of men in OG (olive green) tropical uniform and sat down. I was a bit confused, as they were all talking animatedly but in a language I couldn't make out. Then I noticed their shoulder flashes or insignia, which said 'RWF'. Then the penny dropped – they were Royal Welsh Fusiliers!

At the appointed hour I reported to the Armoury and was issued with a short barrel Lee-Enfield rifle, standard issue for jungle fighting operations, being shorter than the then standard weapon and less cumbersome, and a bandolier of .303 ammunition.

Night train to Kuala Lumpur

Then into a truck and off to the station to report to the OC Troops to be given a berth and then to the Guard Commander to be allotted a time and position for my turn on guard. The train was air conditioned with a foam mattress to sleep on in tiered bunks and very comfortable. The whistle blew and off we went.

The journey was a bit stop and start and the train never got up to any real speed as the route was largely through dense jungle and there was always a danger of animals or trees blocking the track. For my guard duty of two hours I was positioned at the end of one of the carriages by an open window, where I gazed out on the silhouettes of the tree tops in an otherwise inky black jungle, all very exciting! I was relieved eventually but told to keep my weapon with me at all times, which I did, laying it alongside me as I fitfully slept.

At about seven o'clock in the morning we clanked into Kuala Lumpur station and Tommy (Tam) McLean), who had been posted to the same unit, and I disembarked onto the platform, looking rather dishevelled.

21 Air Maintenance Platoon

After a while an RAOC Land Rover appeared to pick us up and take us to our unit. It was the CO's vehicle and the driver was very smart in freshly laundered OGs and he chatted with us as we journeyed through 'KL' to the camp. The camp was on the RAF base at KL Airport, which was also shared with the Air Despatch Unit, 55 Company RASC (AD), and situated near the only runway which was just about big enough to take large passenger airliners, which at that time were all piston-engined. At one end of the runway there was a railway embankment which carried the only line to the north. The embankment was about 40 feet high, so it could be a bit of a hazard for aircraft taking off.

The area around the airport was hilly and covered with tropical vegetation and the whole camp, including RAF personnel, was quite large and covered several acres, although the actual Civil Airport buildings were quite modest, as at that time civilian passenger traffic was very light. Our accommodation was in long wood-framed buildings or 'bashas' as they were called, covered by dry palm or atap leaves at the sides and on the roof so as to keep the huts cool and dry. The interior housed about 30 beds with two lockers or cabinets per bed, one large, one small, and were beside an iron-framed bed with a foam rubber mattress and a mosquito net. It was built with two or three others on the side of a hill so had views out over the airfield and parts of the camp. The camp itself included large warehouse-type sheds in which equipment was stored and prepared for air drop. This was done by packing the various items in small wooden boxes, of which a dozen or so were then strapped together and a parachute harness attached ready for the chute to be clipped on.

The camp also included a cook house and mess tent run by the Army Catering Corps and also ablutions, showers and latrines. There was a Nissen hut style open sided NAAFI operated by Chinese staff and selling beer and snacks. Discretely tucked away was a 'PAC' or prophylactic aid centre, which was a urinal type shed for self-administered treatment by any squaddie who had been with a prostitute. It involved disinfecting soaps and creams and was an attempt to control venereal diseases, which were rife in the region. There was also a resident tailor who had a small shop selling shirts and he could run you up a pair of trousers in a couple of hours from a choice of materials. Outside the shop was a Coke vending machine dispensing ice cold Coke for 20 cents. A 'dhobi' or laundry service was also available at a modest cost.

Within walking distance was the Britannia Club, a social centre for other ranks, which was a brick building containing a small cinema, bar cum cafeteria, snooker and table tennis tables and a very good outdoor swimming pool. We visited this regularly together with other members of the units based on the airfield site, which included a large RAF contingent. It was staffed by local people in conjunction with the WVS (Women's Voluntary Services).

In my unit, 21 Air Maintenance Platoon or 21 AMP, about 35 of us were responsible for the supply of ammunition and equipment to troops operating in the jungle via airdrops. This we did in conjunction with our sister unit 55 Company RASC (Royal Army

Service Corps), who supplied food and fuel and did most if not all of the flying and despatching, although from time to time we also flew with them as dispatchers. The aircraft we used were Vickers Valettas or 'pigs' as they were known, due to their fat fuselage and stubby wings. They were nevertheless very suitable for the job of flying over hilly jungle covered terrain and dropping supplies to the remote jungle DZs or dropping zones. They were flown by the Royal New Zealand or Royal Australian Air Forces as part of the Commonwealth Brigade which was engaged in suppressing the Communist Terrorists or 'CTs'.

Our workplace was a large warehouse where all the equipment was kept and an adjoining small warehouse which contained an admin office with teleprinter and packing area. Weapons and ammunition were kept in a separate facility in a different location, for safety and security reasons. Requests were received from the various units operating in the jungle and were sent to us via the teleprinter, usually overnight, for packing and airdropping the following day. I was told by the Platoon sergeant, Sgt Perkins, that I would be employed as the Platoon clerk assisting with preparing daily orders and general admin and disciplinary matters. So I had a desk in the Platoon office outside the CO, Captain 'Sandy' McGregor's office, and in essence I was a general assistant and occasionally helped out in the warehouse.

On the whole the group was a very friendly one and I soon settled into the daily routine, which also involved camp guard duty and overnight duty in the warehouse keeping an eye on the stores and being available to open up in an emergency. These duties were shared by all personnel on a rota basis.

The main camp guard consisted of an NCO as guard commander and six or seven men to do guard patrols of the camp perimeter each armed with a rifle and ammunition. There was always a spare man in case of sudden illness etc, so the Orderly

Officer inspecting the parade would select the smartest man, who would then be stood down and not required for actual guard duty. This man was known as the 'Stick Orderly' and had to stay on camp to be available if needed. I quickly decided this was for me and always went to great pains with my kit and turnout. This made me successful on many occasions, thus avoiding the tedium of guard duty.

Of course it was very hot and humid, but after a few weeks you became acclimatised as your blood thinned, which could be a nuisance if you got a cut or other wound, as it was difficult to stem the blood. At that time very few places had air conditioning, so you learned to live with it and keep hydrated and take plenty of salt! I remember seeing a squaddie in a terrible state of delirium as a result of salt deficiency. He was lying on his bed writhing and raving and making a hell of a noise – it was quite frightening. But after large doses of salt tablets and a sedative, he was back to normal in a couple of hours.

So there I was at 18 years old guarding the far flung borders of the British Empire!

Thoughts on the British Empire

A lot of nonsense has been spouted in recent times about the evils of empire and colonialism and a distorted and biased view has been espoused by people who had little or no experience of it, together with the actual experiences of some of its former indigenous subjects. Now I'm not going to pretend that atrocities were not committed by us British. The Amritsar massacre in 1919 was a heinous crime, involving the slaughtering of innocent Sikhs peacefully demonstrating by subjecting them to a hail of bullets, killing many. This was a deeply shameful episode for which the senior officer responsible received no punishment other than a reprimand. The Indian Mutiny and its subsequent barbaric suppression was another, although the vile slaughter of white civilians by the mutineers was a considerable provocation, inciting a revenge by the British which was equally bloody, perhaps more. There was also the armed suppression of legitimate freedom fighters in Kenya, Rhodesia and Cyprus, which involved unacceptable treatment of the population including, sadly, torture.

The age of discovery, colonisation and exploitation carried out by European nations was something of its time and is not a phenomenon to be repeated. It was surely inevitable that exploration and expansion would happen, given the insatiable curiosity and greed of Homo sapiens. It could be argued, however, that the investment in, and the creation of indebtedness by, some current major powers, eg China, of Third World countries to gain control of mineral and other strategic assets constitutes in these times a subtler form of 'colonial type' exploitation. One of the major crimes committed by the colonial powers was the appalling practice of slavery, which ultimately resulted in the displacement of millions of people, principally Africans, to America and the West Indies, which has created great resentment by people of colour of white people and vice versa. This will take a long time to finally resolve, but we are, I think getting there, albeit at a very slow pace. The slave trade in the British Empire was abolished in 1807 by Act of Parliament following a campaign by abolitionists. However it did not finally cease until 1838 following the payment of compensation to former slave owners, an understandably very contentious point with former slaves and their descendants.

In the last 80 or so years Britain has more or less divested itself of its vast empire by, mostly, the voluntary granting of independence, sometimes accelerated by armed uprisings, as for example in the cases of Kenya and Rhodesia. The old empire has now morphed into the Commonwealth. comprising most if not all the former colonies plus two or three countries which were never British colonies to form an association of countries with shared values of freedom and justice as well as trade and aid. So the British Empire can surely not have been so heinous, so savagely violent as to be anathema to its former subjects. I will leave this fascinating subject, but it is something one could debate for a very long time.

My experience was very positive and I personally encountered no overt animosity from the Malays, Indians and Chinese who made up the population of Malaya. I find the current unreserved vilification of colonialism and empire very ill informed, bigoted and one sided. If you consider the post-colonial scenario, there is a significant number of former colonies, particularly in Africa, where the population is exploited and the state robbed of money by their unscrupulous 'elected' leaders, and corruption is rife, to the detriment of ordinary people.

I in no way imply that there weren't evils, theft and, sadly, atrocities, committed in the Empire, but on the other hand we left behind the rule of law, infrastructure such as roads, railways etc, language, democracy and technology, not to mention cricket!

The Empire was mostly kept together and ruled by a large civil service, many of whom dedicated their lives to the country in which they served, rather than by force of arms, although the threat was of course always there. The indigenous Indian army far outnumbered the white British one and could have overcome the local white British forces, which is largely what happened in the Indian Mutiny. Consider what might have happened if the European nations had not ventured forth to the rest of the world. That's a very big and fascinating 'what if'. What was it that made the European powers so inquisitive, as opposed to say the African, Asian and South American indigenous peoples? Trade played a large part in it and the Silk Road had been in existence for very many centuries. We know that there were some incidents of explorers from the east venturing west, and famously the Scandinavians were the first to set foot in North America prior to Columbus, but they were isolated incidents, so far as we know. Anyway that's something to ponder on.

Perhaps the biggest crime, or mistake, perpetrated by European colonists was to draw lines on a map to delineate the territory they had seized without any regard to traditional tribal homelands and ethnic borders, an approach which became the root cause of so much of the subsequent conflict in the world. It's a fascinating subject, but obviously the greatest impact by far was as a result of the slave trade, which displaced millions of Africans to the Americas and Caribbean under appalling, inhumane conditions. This is yet another example of man's inhumanity to man, which continues to this day. It should also be borne in mind that at the height of the slave trade in the 18th century, the plight of the average British worker was only a few steps above slavery, being paid a pittance and being disposable at the whim of an employer without any redress.

Slavery was not invented by the British; it is as old as civilisation and continues today, unhappily not least in Africa. It was also a largely British movement, which eventually led to its abolition.

Sadly history is peppered with examples of man's inability to co exist irrespective of race or creed. Who would have believed that in the mid 20th century millions would be slaughtered for being Jewish or for not conforming to the dogma of the Chinese and Russian or Islamic states? It continues to this day in Ukraine, Myanmar, North Korea and elsewhere and is almost wholly due to autocratic dictators drunk on power and greed. I am heartily sick of all the guilt and angst that is presently being exhibited and expressed about Empire and colonialism. I witnessed many examples of genuine warmth and comradeship between European colonists and those they governed or employed.

Anyway, I digress. Back to Malaya, 1957/8.

Daily life in an operational army unit

It was customary for British troops to employ locals to carry out menial tasks in camps, mainly cleaning, and I shared the services of a middle-aged Indian of low caste called Mila who came up to the billet and cleaned it and our kit, for which he was paid a small wage by each squaddie.

Regrettably, Mila was not treated very well by some of my comrades. He suffered a degree of racial abuse and was sometimes not paid for many days. He was about 40, the age of my father, very dark skinned with thinning black hair and of average height and build. He had a pleasant but subservient manner and referred to each of us as 'Boss'. He always wore shorts and a shirt and often padded barefoot around the billet. I felt uncomfortable at the way he was sometimes treated and I always spoke politely to him.

I remember on one occasion coming up from the mess one evening with a mug of tea which I saw him eye covetously, so I offered him a drink from it. He said 'Thank you boss,' and jumped up.

'Here, drink out of this side of the mug,' I said.

'Oh no boss, I get other mug' he replied, jn spite of my insistence.

It suddenly dawned on me that he was not supposed to share an item owned by an upper caste person, so I quickly backed off and poured some tea into his proffered mug, which he took with a short bow and grateful thanks. After that I would on the odd occasion bring him a mug of tea, which he accepted with a beaming smile and thanks.

Then one Thursday evening payday, I was sitting on my bed

reading a magazine and Mila was finishing his work and starting to pack his things up. He walked up to me and said 'You no go out tonight with boys for drink boss?'

'No Mila' I said, 'no money, lost a lot at cards.'

'Oh boss, not good,' he said, nodding his head sagely.

'No,' I said, 'but that's the way it is.'

He walked off, then, a little while later he came up to me. He pressed a handful of Straits dollars into my hand and said, 'You go out have good time, Boss. Pay me back when you can.'

Even now I get a lump in my throat recalling this incident, which taught me an invaluable lesson of life: that if you treat people with decency and respect it will invariably be reciprocated. Thanks Mila!

Leave in Singapore

An opportunity arose for a small group of us to go on a few days' leave to Singapore, and we leapt at the chance. So off we went by train to stay in the Union Jack Club, a hostel providing basic accommodation for British and Commonwealth servicemen and women whilst on 'local' leave.

I particularly remember a visit to the Tiger Balm Gardens, a tropical horticultural garden sponsored by Tiger Balm, a hugely popular Chinese therapeutic ointment. The gardens are amazing and well worth a visit being a sort of tropical Kew Gardens.

One evening four of us ventured down town to the dock area on the approach road, to see was a large sign which read 'Out of Bounds to All Service Personnel'. However after a very brief chat and filled with the Dutch courage induced by a few pints of Tiger Beer, we said 'bugger it, let's explore', and off we went.

Now as there was a group of us we were probably quite safe. The area was a hot spot for Chinese criminal gangs who could be quite ruthless, but they were inevitably not keen to harm squaddies in view of the drastic response this would inevitably provoke. The area was a hotbed of drug dealing and prostitution run by the gangs in 'territories', but its attraction to us was the fantastic variety of superb, cheap Chinese restaurants which mainly catered for the coolies working the docks. Many of these were on the pavement and were dwarfed by the enormous dockside warehouses or 'godowns' as they were called, Indian English for warehouse. We alighted on one, but of course no English was spoken and the menu was in Chinese. However we got by with the usual banter and joking with the waiter and managed to order a feast for next to nothing.

One of the dishes they served up was in fact a Malay dish, satay, a sauce which could be mild or hot in which you dipped meat kebabs. It was our first experience of it and our waiter was smiling and saying 'you eat, you eat, velly velly good'! I decided Id take the plunge and show the others, so I picked up a bamboo splinter of small chicken kebab, dipped it in the satay sauce and took a mouthful. There was a brief lull and then my mouth felt like it was ablaze and I urgently demanded water or beer to quench the burning sensation, all much to the amusement of the local Chinese eating there. The waiter suddenly appeared with what looked like a small plate of cucumber and urged me to chew that, not drink, which I did. Sure enough it worked and the flames in my mouth were extinguished!

I'm still not sure that was actually satay, it was so hot. Maybe it was a case of 'lost in translation'.

Also in our party was a fellow squaddie of Chinese parentage but from Liverpool, one Ricky Chin, and we asked him if he could act as interpreter. but he said 'No mate. don't speak the lingo'! Even if he had done I doubt the locals would have understood him with his very broad scouse accent!

Another favourite destination for a day out was Port Dickson on the coast south of Kuala Lumpur and now a popular holiday destination. It was, as far as I remember, about a two-hour drive from our camp and the road took you through hilly country via the Seremban Pass. This had been a favourite spot for terrorists to ambush and rob travellers and the army, so we had to go armed. It was not a particularly high risk route as terrorist activity at that time was extremely low, but nevertheless we took our weapons just in case.

At that time there was very little in the way of facilities at 'PD', as it was known, so we took some food and a frying pan and had a cook up at midday . There were excellent sandy beaches and the sea was warm, so we swam and generally messed around, although we were warned to watch out for sea snakes! Later, while talking to an RAF helicopter pilot in Singapore, he said he'd made a number of low altitude flights down the coast during which he had witnessed the sea life. His opinion was that after the things he'd seen swimming in that stretch of water, in no way would you get him to swim in it!

One rather sad phenomenon was the groups of apparently orphaned or homeless children who would appear, especially if there was any food around, and our culinary efforts on the beach attracted about half a dozen youngsters of both Chinese and Malay ethnicity, both girls and boys. Needless to say we always gave them something to eat and had a laugh and joke with them. I was given to understand that they were mostly war orphans from the Japanese occupation in World War 2, but how true this was I can't say.

Unit group photograph, Kuala Lumpur Airfield 1957

Valetta aircraft coming into land at "KL" after an airdrop

Typical jungle dropping zone or 'DZ'

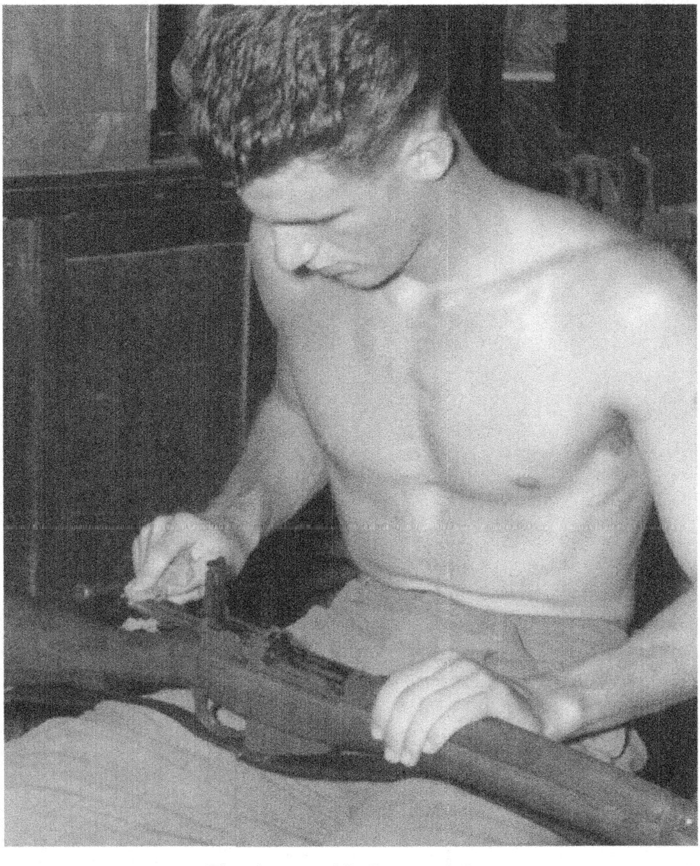

Cleaning my rifle for guard duty

Inside our" basha"

The outside of the "basha"

Ready for guard duty outside the "basha"

Squatting in front of my bedside locker

Being talked to by the Brigadier heading up the inspection team

Having a fry- up on the beach at Port Dickson with Fraser Clarke

Jamming with pal on camp

A Malaysian krait

CHAPTER 9

Adventures in Malaya

'KL'

Kuala Lumpur was a pleasant colonial type city with some attractive buildings and gardens, standing on the Klang River. At that time it was heaving with military, mainly army and air force, and while the majority were from UK there was a large contingent from Australia, New Zealand and of course the wonderful Gurkhas. All of us got along pretty well and in all we constituted 'The Commonwealth Brigade'. The Gurkhas have fought as an integral part of the British Army for around 200 years and the reason this came about is interesting. In the early 19th century, Britain invaded Nepal, the Gurkha State, as part of the plan to conquer Northern India. However the Gurkhas, although outgunned by the British, refused to give in and fought with such tenacity as to greatly impress the British military high command. As a result, peace was agreed and the Gurkhas were incorporated within the British Army, where they have ever since been a potent and revered fighting force. It is an interesting but odd fact that the Gurkhas are the only unit in the British Army that allows alcoholic spirits to be served in the other ranks mess (Gurkha rum).

On pay nights it was the general thing to go into town and drink in the bars and then have a meal, usually a curry or Chinese or Malay food, and generally fraternise. I well remember, among many incidents, one night when I got in with a bunch of New Zealanders, or Kiwis, which included some Maori soldiers, one of whom, by the name of Kaga, had somehow got hold old of a big old American Oldsmobile sedan to travel around in. Now this particular night when we were all pretty sloshed, Kaga insisted on driving to the curry house in his car. When we had all piled in, Kaga, who was very drunk, said he couldn't see the road properly and as I was in the front next to him he instructed me to be his eyes and say 'Kaga go', 'Kaga stop', 'Kaga left', 'Kaga right'! Needless to say it was a short but hairy trip, albeit at little more than walking pace, but we arrived in one piece. He was a big tough lad but very likeable and had quite a laid-back nature.

Another memorable night among many was when a few of us visited the BK Bar, a Chinese-owned restaurant cum bar in KL. Now this bar had been adopted by the SAS, who did not like any other units using it and would quickly turf out any interlopers. However our unit was tolerated, because we did their air supply and bent the rules a bit for them from time to time like sticking six packs of beer in with the equipment drops. On this particular evening there were a number of SAS lads just out from a couple of weeks in the jungle and celebrating in the usual way and I perhaps should also mention here that the BK bar also incorporated a brothel! Anyway, somehow or other they decided to have a jousting competition whereby two SAS troopers would each have one of us mounted on their shoulders with a fluorescent tube as a lance and charge each other to try and dismount the opponent. The fluorescent tubes were extracted from the restaurant lighting, wrapped with a tunic top and hey presto. Complete bloody madness, but there you are, that's how it was. Boys will be boys!

Happily it didn't last too long as the Chinese owner pleaded with us to please desist, as someone could get a nasty cut and he would lose his tubes, so I, being one of the 'jockeys' survived. And yes, the tubes were replaced intact!

At the other end of the spectrum, there were a couple of semi-feral Golden Retrievers roaming about the camp, probably abandoned by NCOs or officers returning home or posted away. Anyway one bitch suddenly produced five pups, which were instantly adopted by all and sundry and were fed generously at the cookhouse door.

A desperate situation arose one afternoon when the dogs and pups appeared covered in tar from nose to tail, a sorry sight indeed. They had evidently strayed onto a section of the camp road which was being tarred and chipped by a road repair gang. The CSM (Company Sergeant Major) and CO said they should be put down in view of their dreadful state, which would make it difficult for them to survive, given they were trying to lick the tar off. But, to a man, the two units ourselves and 55 Company lads weren't having it and a rescue method was quickly improvised. This involved first wiping the tar off with cotton waste soaked in high octane aviation gasoline and next passing them over to another team who trimmed off the hair where it was too thickly stuck on Then another team shampooed them to get rid of any tar residue and towelled them dry. Now Av Gas is very high octane and if your skin is exposed to it for too long it can burn, so the guys doing that part of the cleaning had to constantly stop and rinse their hands and the dogs and pups to stop them being burned.

It turned out later that a sergeant who had been instructed to put the pups down with a .38 revolver got to the stage of loading the gun and pointing it at one of the pup's heads which then wagged its tail and tried to lick the gun. This was too much for the sergeant, who said he just couldn't do it!

They all made a good recovery, but the CO said homes must be found for them and this was eventually done, although one of the older dogs stayed on camp, having been unofficially adopted by a tough Geordie corporal. I well remember the time he was demobbed. He sat on the back of the truck taking him to the station in tears as his dog followed him out the camp, so it then had to be caught and brought back.

While there I experienced what the Army calls an 'Admin Inspection' when the whole camp were subjected to a physical inspection by an officer of field rank and his team of four or five officers and senior NCOs. The object is to ensure that everything is clean and in good order and functioning properly. Needless to say this entails a considerable amount of 'bull' and everything, and I do mean everything, gets cleaned and polished and brought up to the highest standard and the officer commanding the unit rated accordingly. Thus in the weeks before the inspection there is a mad panic to get every thing looking spick and span. Things get taken to extremes in an effort to make certain all is as good as it can be, and sometimes this can border on the farcical.

In this particular case, it was noted on the eve of the inspection that the grass outside our Company Office was too long and I was instructed, together with Tommy McLean, to cut it down to an inch all over. So believe it or not Tommy and I found ourselves on our hands and knees with a large pair of scissors and a ruler each cutting the grass to regulation length. How barmy is that? But it gets better (or worse). It was late afternoon and twilight in the tropics is of very brief duration, so we quickly found ourselves in near darkness with the job only half done and the inspection due to start early next morning. We pointed this out to our Sergeant, 'Polly' Perkins, who immediately ordered the duty driver to bring a three-ton truck around and position it so he could illuminate the grass with its headlights. So there we were on our hands and knees cutting the grass with scissors and a ruler to measure the right height, and all by the headlights of a three-ton truck!

The inspection duly went ahead and was considered a success. During it I was addressed by the Colonel leading the inspection team, who asked me how I liked National Service and what my job was in civvy street etc. There's a photo of this event in the archive.

Also during the proceedings our 'Basha', or living quarters, was inspected, including a full kit layout. Now the buildings we slept in, our home, were constructed using a wooden frame covered by woven atap grass, a sort of palm leaf. This was perfectly weatherproof and had the great advantage of keeping the interior cool. But the atap grass attracted 'chit-chats', small newt-sized lizards, which lived in the roofing area. They were protected by military law and it was an offence to harm one as they helped to keep the insect life under control, including mosquitoes.

So there we all were standing to attention by our beds when the Colonel's party trooped in. The one drawback to chit-chats was their toilet habits, which resulted in them scattering their poo all over the place. This was not a problem as it consisted of tiny pinhead sized balls of solid matter and one simply brushed it away, it wasn't excessive and you lived with it. But by the time the inspection occurred a visible amount had accumulated in small areas. This was seen by a hawk-eyed sergeant in the party, who drew attention to it. 'What's this?' asked the Colonel.

'Lizard droppings,' volunteered our CO.

'Oh, you mean shit,' said the Colonel.

'Well yes sir,' said our man, looking a tad embarrassed.

We were all convulsed and desperately trying not to laugh. A bit juvenile I know, but it broke the tension of a somewhat trying situation.

Jungle patrol

To defeat the Communist Terrorists (CTs) or Malayan Races Liberation Army, which was were backed by the Chinese Communist Government, a plan was drawn up to divide Malaya into kilometre squares, which were all coloured black, assuming terrorist activity. As the CTs were flushed out of a square it was declared 'white', signifying it was clear of CT activity. Regular infantry regiments were used for the initial clearance, and these included Kings Own Scottish Borderers, Durham Light Infantry, The Green Jackets, Gurkhas and SAS. But in order to prevent any re-incursion, support troops such as RASC, RAOC, Royal Signals, REME etc were drafted in to do follow up patrols in order to 'show the flag' and let any CTs who might be lying low know that the army was in control.

Thus it came to pass that I found myself taking part in a 48-hour jungle patrol. We were designated an area not too far away and the platoon, in full combat gear, was dropped off at a point on the edge of some dense jungle and rubber plantations.

We advanced in the prescribed manner as taught in our basic training, and ventured further and further into some pretty thick jungle. I loved it, as it was real soldiering and the jungle was alive all around us with the cries of birds, the chatter of monkeys and some pretty gigantic insects. I remember creeping under some foliage and suddenly coming face to face with a large spider's web with the owner at home. It was jet black with long legs which extended would overlap a saucer in circumference, and the lower part of its body was vivid emerald green. Quite a sight, so I very, very carefully navigated around it!

Eventually, it was time to make camp, which we did on the edge of a rubber plantation. We were staking out our sleeping areas and starting to break out our ration packs when some small arms fire broke out quite near. Immediately we assumed defensive positions with loaded weapons and waited anxiously for what would happen next. A couple of scouts were sent out to recce the area and after a while they returned with nothing to report, so we posted guards and ate our rations in shifts. I slept that night near a large bamboo clump cuddling my rifle, but had a reasonable sleep in the circumstances.

Shortly after daybreak we continued our patrol and after a while came to some very thick vegetation which necessitated taking to a large stream which we waded up, water well above our waists, holding our weapons and ammo above our heads. When we reached less dense terrain we climbed out of the stream and checked each other for leeches. We found plenty on our bodies. These were removed by holding a cigarette close to them and when they retracted their proboscis, flicking them off. As a precaution we were advised beforehand to wear tight fitting pants or swimming briefs to avoid the chance of getting a leech in your willy or bum!

Finally the patrol ended when we reached a Malayan Police post on the edge of the jungle or 'Ulu' in local jargon. The post was memorable for having a geothermal swimming pool fed by a hot spring and we all had a wonderful dip in it. We also learned that the small arms fire we had experienced was from a Malayan Police unit patrolling the same area who had ceased fire after they checked and found out it was an army unit. It could have been worse, but just shows how easily 'friendly fire' incidents can happen. All in all a memorable experience.

As a postscript, I learned subsequently that it is not advisable to sleep near bamboo clumps as these are the favourite nesting sites for snakes, of which Malaya has its share of some pretty poisonous ones!

Independence, or 'merdeka'

On the 31st August 1957 Malaya became an independent nation, which naturally involved a great day of national celebration. There was some uncertainty among the Malayan hierarchy as to how this might turn out, given that both the Chinese and Indian communities were quite large and dominated the banking and commercial life of Malaya and would now be subject to the rule of the indigenous Malays. So to be prepared for any trouble, the police and army would provide riot control duties. This entailed covering the windows on army lorries with protective wire mesh and providing army personnel with batons. Thus some of us were placed on standby.

Happily the whole thing passed off peacefully and Malaya transitioned smoothly from colony to independent nation, to everyone's relief and satisfaction. It was agreed that British forces would remain for the time being to finish the job of expelling the CTs from the country, which had in any case almost been accomplished. Then there would be a phased withdrawal, which duly took place. Apropos of this it was interesting that in spite of the large Chinese and Indian elements of Malayan society, there was practically no inter-marriage and each ethnic group kept themselves to themselves, including the Malay, with little or no interracial strife.

Life continued quite unaffected by political events, but one Wednesday afternoon our peace and quiet was shattered by the sound of some very large military aircraft coming in to land We all got up and stood outside our Bashas to watch three mighty American C119C military transport aircraft come in to land. The runway at KL was not that long, but they were designed to land on short runways. The purpose of the visit was a liaison with British Air Supply Units to compare notes, and we were invited to visit the aircraft and crews, which we did enthusiastically and received a friendly greeting from the American airmen, who showed us over their aircraft. At that time we were the only fully operational active service air supply unit in the world, so they were interested to meet and talk with us. They only stayed a short while and were gone the next day.

Then some weeks later an air drop competition was held on the Thai border: British crews versus Americans. Evidently the Americans won on the basis that they delivered more equipment on the Dropping Zone. Bearing in mind their aircraft could carry several times our Valetta's payload, we thought this was a bit unfair, as in any case our drops, percentage wise, got more on the actual DZ. Just as a passing comment, on the camp we had two Army Catering Corps cooks who were regularly seen walking hand in hand. When anyone commented on this, the usual casual response was 'Oh they're nancy boys', and the conversation moved on. This was in retrospect extraordinary, given that at that time homosexuality was a Court Martial offence punishable with a prison sentence and a dishonourable discharge. Strange!

Snakes alive!

I mentioned that Malaya had its fair share of poisonous reptiles. A hilarious but scary episode involving a krait, one of the most poisonous snakes in the world, took place one evening during the monsoon season. The monsoon delivers enormous amounts of rain, usually in our case starting at around 4 pm and lasting several hours. Quite often you could have a shower in it, and it was great for shampoos as the rainwater was so soft. However snakes do not like to get too wet, so they seek cover! Three or four of us came back to our Basha one night after a few beers in the NAAFI hut and didn't switch all he lights on so as not to disturb anyone asleep.

Lou Costello, a lorry driver from West Ham, had a bed at the far end of the billet and as he approached his bed he found to his horror a metre and a half krait curled up asleep between his bed and the side of the Basha, He cried out in a hushed voice to warn us and beat a hasty retreat to where the rest of us were standing. After a brief discussion we decided to see if we could get it to go away, so we crept down to his bed and viewed in awe this beautiful but deadly snake curled up, obviously oblivious to our presence. Lou, against our advice, decided that the only thing to do was to drop his small bedside locker on it to kill it. So with us trying to persuade him otherwise, he stood on his bed, picked up the locker, aimed and dropped it from a height of about four feet onto the unsuspecting snake.

Unfortunately we had all overlooked the fact that the locker had about a three inch beading gap underneath it to raise it off the ground, so it didn't touch the snake but aroused it from its slumbers, upon which, with ominous hisses, it started to slither across the floor towards us. There was a blind panic to get out of the billet, and we stayed out for about half an hour before very cautiously creeping back. After a very careful search without finding any sign of our visitor we gingerly climbed into bed, securing our mosquito nets around us just in case.

I afterwards learned that kraits are common throughout Asia and India and that a number of the unexplained deaths earlier in the 20th century are now thought to have been due to kraits, which would slither into buildings at night and sometimes into beds and bite you. The symptoms were evidently akin to heart failure, which was concluded to have been the cause of death, so no one therefore bothered to look for bite marks, which in any case were quite small and indistinct, although the venom causes paralysis and, if untreated, death. Indeed there is a BBC film about this.

As an aside, I found the wildlife in Malaya amazing and

fascinating. I recall another event in the monsoon season when from the extensive swathes of grass around our billets literally millions of large flies suddenly seemed to erupt, flying straight up into the sky, where birds and bats, also in great numbers, were circling for a feed. At the same time frogs and toads appeared in force and devoured those about to take off. An astounding example of nature 'red in tooth and claw'!

Mosquitoes of course were a problem to begin with and the advised dress code from dusk onwards was long trousers and sleeves. We also each had a 'mozzy' net which could be slung above your bed and tucked in all around to protect you while sleeping. Malaria was of course the big danger and we all took Paludrine tablets, an anti malarial drug. However the little chit-chats helped to keep the mozzies under control and there was regular spraying of any standing water on or near the camp to destroy the larvae.

It was said that mosquitoes wouldn't bother you if you had had a couple of beers and I certainly found this to be true, enabling you to sleep without a net. It was believed that the smell of beer on your breath repelled mosquitoes. Many years later I read an article from a medic which stated that it was indeed true that drinking beer was a deterrent to mosquitoes, but not from your breath; it was due to the yeast in the beer being exuded in the body's normal perspiration. It recommended taking yeast tablets as a precaution before visiting countries where mosquitoes and malaria were a problem.

Also there were the amazing praying mantises, spindly insects about four or five inches long whose name derives from their posture of drawing their upper limbs together under their heads as if praying. I used to have one come and sit on the edge of my mug of tea, and if a mosquito came buzzing near, the Mantis' limbs would shoot out like lightning and grab the mozzy, which it would instantly devour. I well remember one of our cooks got dressed up to go to KL for a night out and out of the blue found a mantis standing on the shoulder of the shirt he was wearing. Unperturbed, the cook went out to some bars and a curry house and returned some hours later with the mantis still on his shoulder!

While on the subject of insects, another one we frequently encountered was the 'flying frog', as we called it. This was a large beetle about the size of a stag beetle but green and although quite harmless, a bit off-putting. Cicadas of course were ever present and they started buzzing as soon as the sun set. It was somehow a relaxing sound and although ever present after dark, not intrusive. One of their chief attributes was that they immediately stopped buzzing if anything large approached them. For this reason, if you were on guard you soon knew if anyone was coming near you, so it was good for security!

Sports day

Sport was very much encouraged, and a variety of sports including rugby and soccer were played around the Kuala Lumpur garrison. We had a rugby side and an athletics team, which I joined as a potential 'miler'. We trained under a young New Zealand Second Lieutenant and went on training runs three mornings a week. This entailed running about three miles over sand dunes and rough ground in a T-shirt, shorts and plimsolls and carrying on our backs a small haversack containing two house bricks. I have certainly never since been as fit as I was then!

Eventually we competed against other units in the Garrison Athletic Championships, where I ran the mile around a grass course at 3.30 in the afternoon – quite hot! I finished a creditable seventh or eighth out of twenty-plus in a time of 4 minutes 35, not a bad time then.

At the end of the day, just as we were leaving the ground, a

Colonel started shouting at us and as he was some distance away was difficult to hear clearly. The Aussie Lieutenant in charge of us kept putting his hand to his ear and shouted back 'Can't hear you sir.' One of our number said to him 'I think he wants us to help with the clearing up sir,' to which the Aussie officer replied 'I know that mate, that's why I can't hear him, now quick as you like on the wagon and lets bugger off!'

Monkey business

One morning our Platoon Sergeant, with whom I worked, said 'Faulder, I understand you like animals?' To which I replied, 'Yes Sarge, very much'.

'Good, you can look after my monkeys over the next week while I'm on leave,' he said.

Evidently he had been more or less ordered to look after two monkeys by an officer but it clashed with his leave. Don't ask me why there were pet monkeys belonging to an officer as I never got to the bottom of it. Anyway the monkeys were kept in a small shed on camp. They were small macaques and were more than a handful, being very crafty and of course very athletic. Most of the time they were in a large cage and really all I had to do was feed them twice a day on various fruits and nuts. So I had quite a laugh with them, although you had to watch out as they had a bit of a bite. I had a lot of squaddies and senior ranks wanting to see them, which made me feel like a zoo keeper!

Reflections on National Service

One of the interesting things about National Service was that it didn't matter who or what you were, once in the services you were thrown together in a unit and subject to military law and its attendant statute 'Queen's Regulations', a document which effectively contains the rules and instructions for running and administering the forces. Now military law is of necessity more direct and stricter than civilian criminal law and there is virtually no court of appeal. One of my jobs was to draw up formal charges for any soldier committing an offence, which I found quite interesting. It was an interesting sociological experience to throw disparate people together all subject to a strict legal system. If you were given an order by a senior rank you obeyed it to the letter or were guilty of an offence. Thus in my unit there was a dustman from Manchester, a steel worker from Sheffield, a coalminer from Fife, a farm labourer from Hertfordshire, a solicitor's clerk from Birmingham, a lorry driver from West Ham, and more of the same, a variety of different trades and social backgrounds. But everyone mucked in and there was little if any falling out. We realised we had to 'get on with it', so all in all it was something of a 'life class'. As I say, an interesting situation.

Flying ops

I did get the opportunity to fly on jungle air drops, which was both exciting and fascinating. To fly you were kitted out with a sort of black boiler suit and issued with a.38 revolver in a holster on your belt, a survival ration pack, and of course jungle boots and beret. The packs for dropping were taken down to the airfield by three-ton trucks and loaded onto the aircraft by a despatching team of usually three or four men. The aircraft were Vickers-Armstrong Valettas, the military version of the Viking, a small airliner of about 50 seats. The Valettas of course were stripped out to accommodate the cargo, except for a few seats for the dispatch crew. They were piloted by Royal Australian Air Force or Royal New Zealand Air Force personnel as part of the Commonwealth Brigade. The packs were ejected manually out of the port side of the aircraft, where there was a large permanently open door. On approaching the drop zone (DZ), the pack was manhandled onto a wooden pallet with handles and at the appropriate time the inboard side of the pallet was lifted to slide the pack into the slipstream. Prior to this the static line had been clipped to a rail inside the plane. Once the pack was clear of the plane the static line pulled the parachute undone and it unfurled (hopefully). The dispatcher hanging slightly out of the aircraft watched it all the way down and advised the pilot by helmet intercom of where it landed so he could calculate future drop times/positions depending on the wind and how near the pack landed to the DZ marker.

The dispatchers were supposed to keep themselves attached to rigging lines in the aircraft to avoid being sucked or falling out, but as this was a bit restricting most just hung on to anything nearby. Having completed the equipment/ammunition drop it was not unusual to do a PW (psychological warfare) leaflet drop. The leaflets, normally just a cartoon depiction of the enemy with a brief disparaging caption, were just heaved out through the open door of the aircraft and fluttered to earth, having been scattered by the slipstream.

While I was in Malaya my parents had my alto sax shipped out to me and I was able to practise in the AD (Air Despatch) shed. While I was having a blow one evening a young RASC squaddie came around and asked if he could join me on trumpet, to which I readily agreed, and we had some pleasant evenings jamming together. Also, because I had served in an active service war zone, I was awarded a medal! It was the General Service Medal or GSM with clasp Malaya. This is also in the archive box.

CHAPTER 10

Back home

Demob time

My two years' National Service was coming to an end and it was time to leave Malaya to return to the UK for demobilisation back into civvy street and resume my career in the insurance industry. Eventually the day came for me to depart, but not without some regrets, as on the whole I had enjoyed my time in Malaya; it had been a very formative experience at a crucial time in my life.

I made my way with some other squaddies to Singapore to embark on the TT *Oxfordshire*, a much more modern and better equipped ship than the old *Dunera* I had come out on. This time however I was berthed on the troop decks but these were, so far as I remember, less confined than the *Dunera*'s. Coming out I had had a birthday at sea and now going back I would have a Christmas at sea. Every effort had been made to make it as festive as possible and we had a very good Christmas lunch. Much to my surprise I received a telegram from my parents wishing me a Happy Christmas. I also managed to get permission to go down into one of the cargo holds to play my sax, but all in all it was a fairly uneventful journey back, although this time we went via the Suez Canal, which had now reopened. This was a fascinating experience as the canal in places is quite narrow and you are surrounded by large sand dunes, which at times you almost appeared to be sailing on. In view of the delicate political situation we wore civvies while on open decks so as not to antagonise the Egyptians, who sadly had had a rough time during the brief invasion by the British and French following Colonel Nasser's seizure of the canal a couple of years earlier.

There was plenty of local activity along the banks of the canal and I remember a group of officers' wives leaning on the rail taking in the scenery and atmosphere when a group of Egyptian men appeared on the bank in their traditional *burnous* garments and started shouting suggestive abuse at them. This culminated in the men lifting their robes and waving their erections at the ladies, who while outwardly expressing disgust with their hands over their eyes, were doing so through open fingers in order not to miss anything! We cruised on out into the Mediterranean, which was a bit choppy, and our final port of call was Gibraltar.

The 'Rock' is a slightly odd place. It's a thin peninsula that stands in a very strategic position at the mouth of the Mediterranean sea but joined to the Spanish mainland. It was ceded to Great Britain by the Treaty of Utrecht in 1713 following the War of the Spanish Succession, a European conflict. It is mostly a very large chunk of rock which stands like a sentinel guarding the Straits of Gibraltar, hence its strategic importance.

We were granted shore leave for the day and set off to explore the town. After visiting various bars, a group of four or five of us finished up in a bar near the quay for a final beer before embarking. We were sitting around a large circular table with two or three others, all in our khaki battledress uniforms. As we were chatting, I noticed that one of the other group at the table was a softly spoken Scot of about 40 with an array of medal ribbons, one of which was the 8th Army Star, indicating that he had been one of the famous 'Desert Rats', as Rommel called them, and had repulsed the might of the German Afrika Corps.

As we sat downing the last of our beers, in stormed the Military Police to clear everybody out to rejoin the ship. MPs have a somewhat menacing appearance in their pristine uniforms, made the more so by their peaked caps, which almost covered their eyes. They are certainly not to be argued with. An MP walked up to our table, banged his cane on it and said 'Right, on your way, NOW', so we shuffled reluctantly to our feet, all except for the ex-Desert Rat, who ignored the MP and carried on defiantly drinking his beer. The MP again whacked his cane on the table and said 'That means you too, soldier'. The old soldier slowly lowered his glass, looked up at the MP and said 'Son, Rommel couldn't shift me so what fucking chance do you think you've got?' and took another sip. The MP paused to consider, then said 'In that case, in your own time soldier', at which the old Desert Rat stood up, smiled and walked slowly to the door. A flicker of a smile passed over the MP's face as he followed us out. 'That was respect,' said one of our party, and it sure was.

We were, of course, coming from hot humid Malaya to cold wet England in February and I recall standing on the deck one morning as we sailed up the English Channel and suddenly hearing over the ship's Tannoy the voice of a BBC announcer introducing the 9 o'clock news. I was home!

Amazingly we had to go through customs, which was a drag, but eventually we boarded lorries to take us back to Blackdown Camp, where, being February, it was bitterly cold with a thin covering of snow and ice on the ground. Quite a difference! There we idled away for two or three weeks pending release from service, although we were automatically entered onto the roll of the Army Emergency Reserve, from which for a period of years we could be called up in the event of a military emergency.

That evening I rang my parents and had a chat with them, making arrangements to go home on a 48-hour leave and bring my pal Tommy McLean to stay with us. This was because it would have taken Tommy a whole day to get back to his home in Dumbarton, by which time it would be time to return.

So it was I arrived back home in Norbury. It was strange to be back. Everything seemed the same as I remembered but somehow or other it wasn't. It was an odd feeling, but maybe it was because I had changed. I was certainly more worldly-wise and confident, as if I had passed through a rite of passage.

About a fortnight later we were finally processed and demobbed from the army. I returned home and contacted my employers to arrange for my return to work. It was all rather strange to be a civilian again. People say that we should bring back National Service, which finally ended in 1960, and indeed some countries do have systems of compulsory military service, but I'm not sure it would work in this day and age in the UK.

I am certainly glad I had the experience, and I gained a great deal from it. Among the many benefits were that I became more confident and self-sufficient, achieved a better understanding of people of all races, experienced mixing with different cultures and saw a large piece of the world at the Government's expense. Also, having served in the army, I came to understand its psyche and what makes it the efficient, professional organisation it is. Unless you have served and experienced it you can only have the vaguest notion of its workings and how it regards itself. When I see that a Government Minister of Defence has been appointed with no service experience, I fail to see how he can carry out his duties effectively and earn respect from the armed forces without the insight that comes from having been a member.

So, now it was back to building a career, and who knows what?

Printed in Great Britain
by Amazon

46544129R00081